Street Atlas of
NORWIC

C000244050

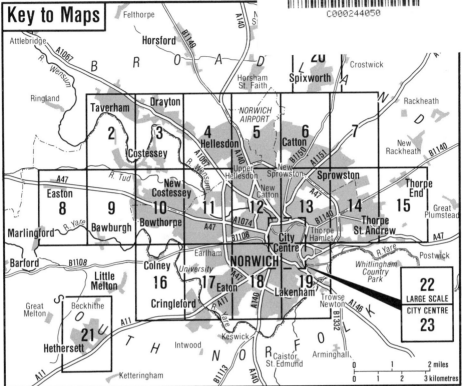

Key to Maps

Reference

EDITION 1

Road	**A47**
Road	**B1149**
ual Carriageway	
e Way Street (raffic flow on A Roads indicated a heavy line on the drivers' left)	→
ailway — Level Crossing — Station	
SCALE 4 inches to 1 mile	

District Boundary	— · — · —
Ambulance Station	✚
Car Parks (Selected)	P
Church or Chapel	✛
Fire Station	■
Hospital	Ⓗ

House Numbers (Selected Roads)	2 — 23
Information Centre	🛈
National Grid Reference	623
Police Station	▲
Post Office	●
Toilet	▽

1:15,840

Geographers' A-Z Map Company Limited

Head Office: Vestry Road, Sevenoaks, Kent, TN14 5EP. Telephone 0732 451152
Showrooms: 44 Gray's Inn Road, Holborn, London, WC1X 8LR. Telephone 01 242 9246

ISBN 0 85039 196 2

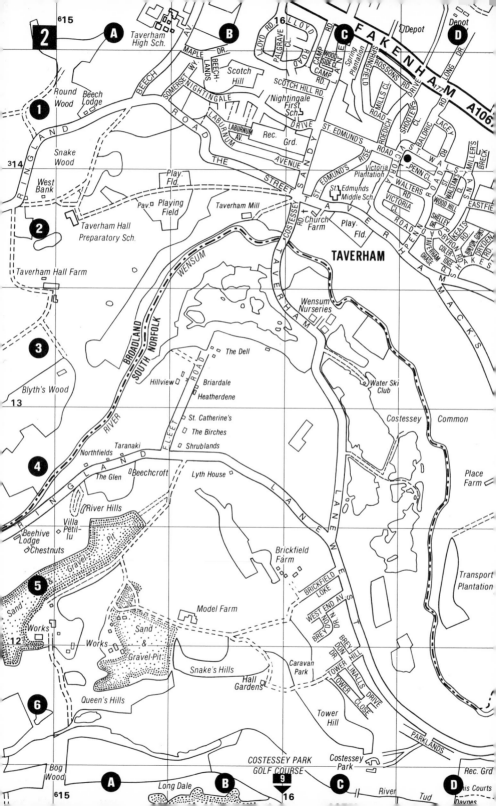

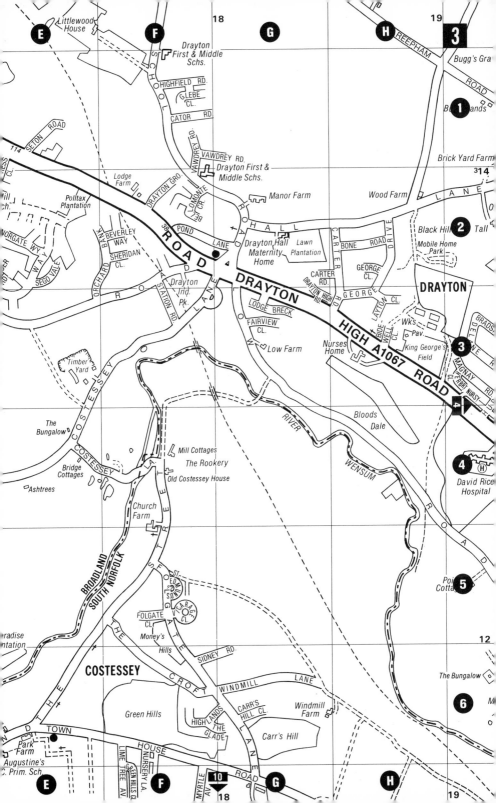

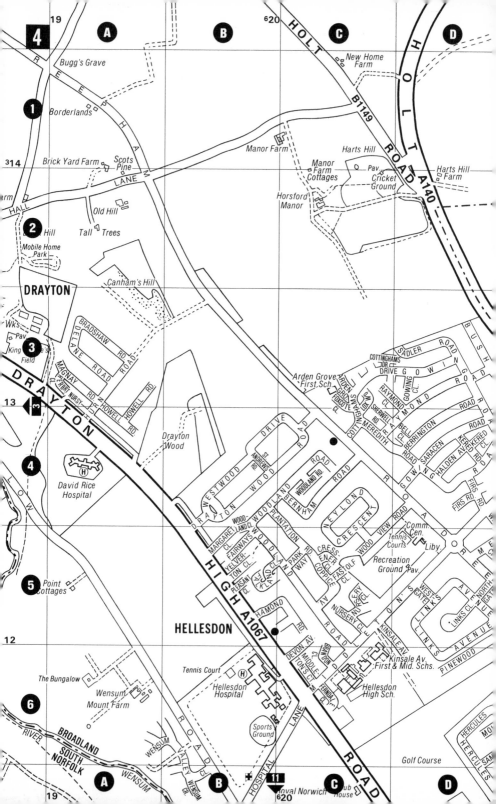

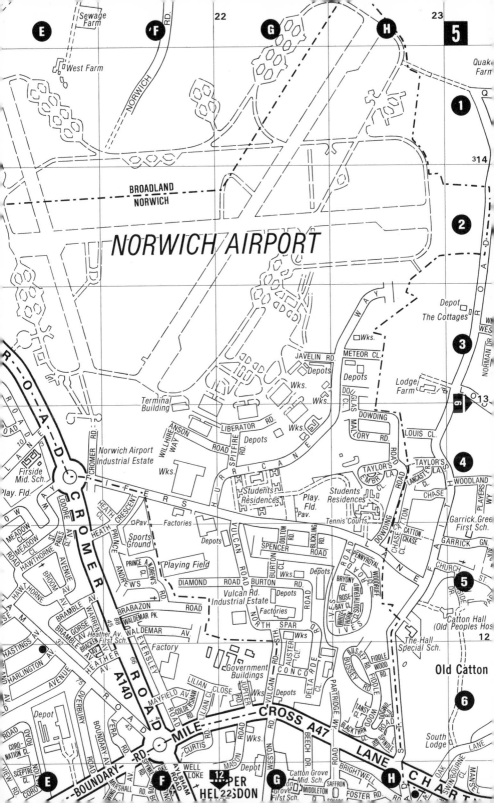

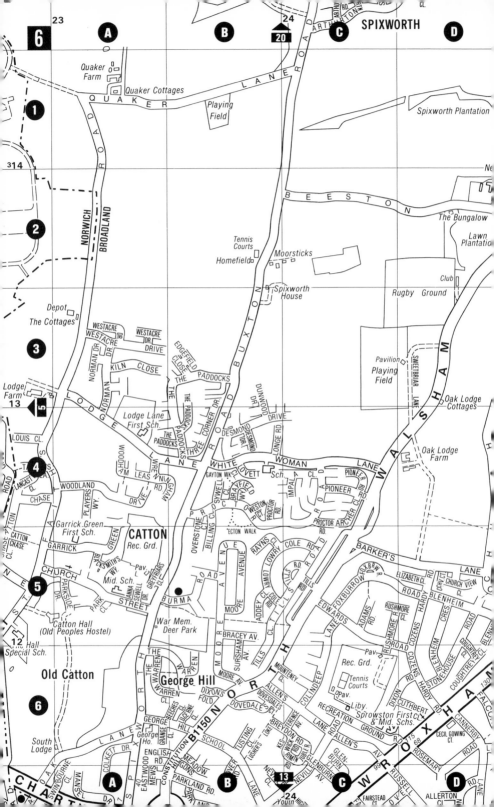

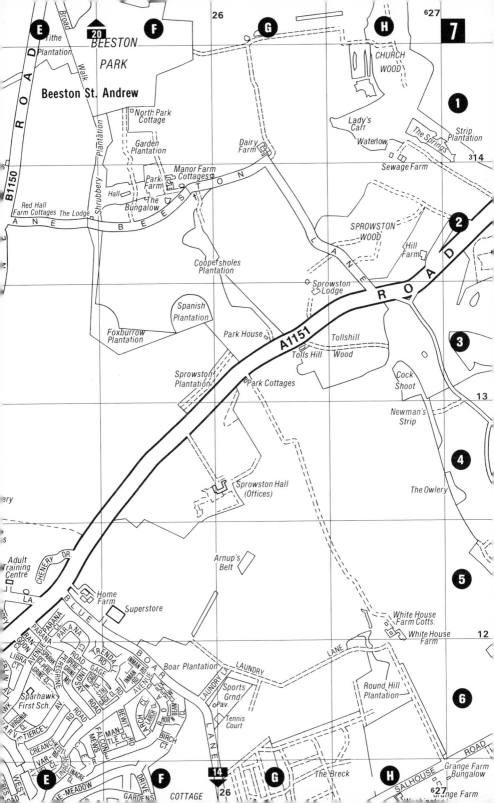

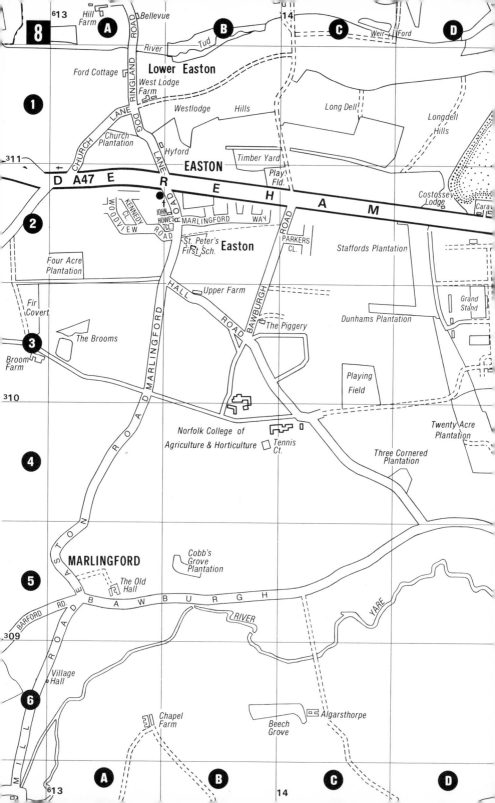

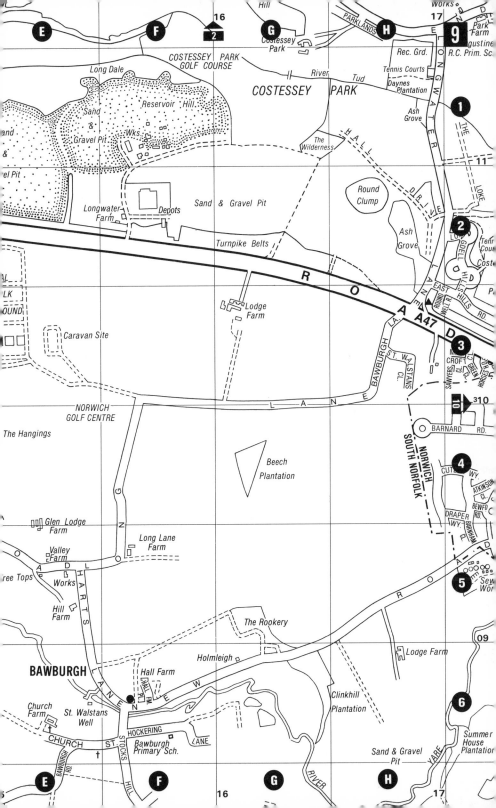

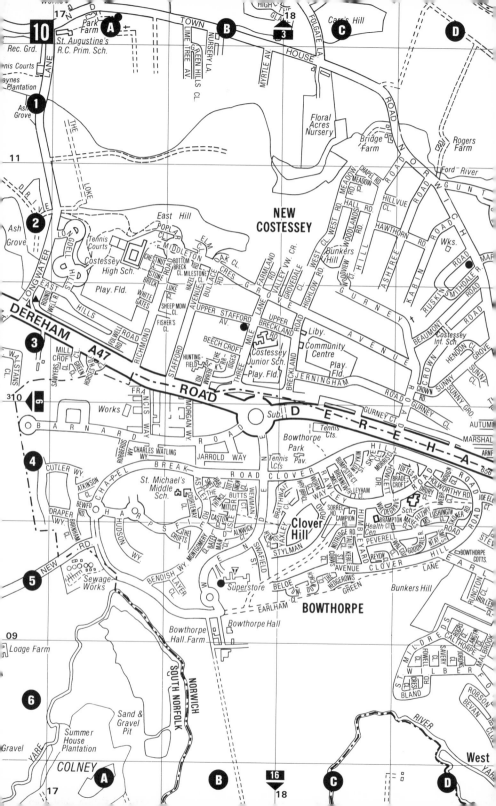

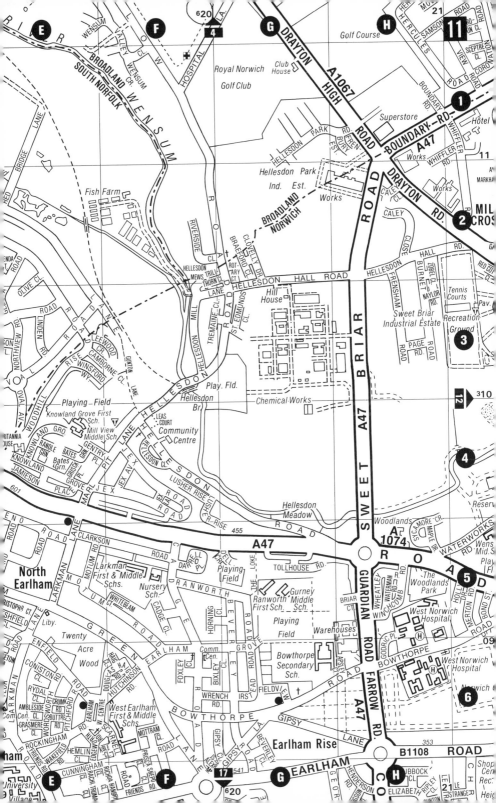

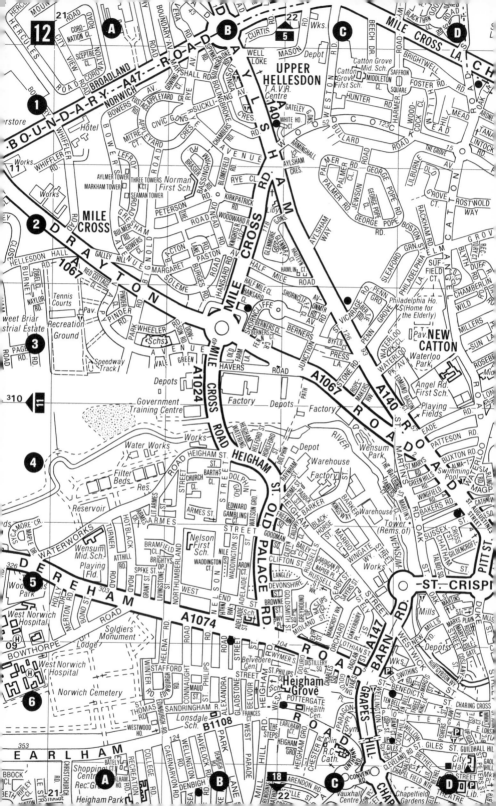

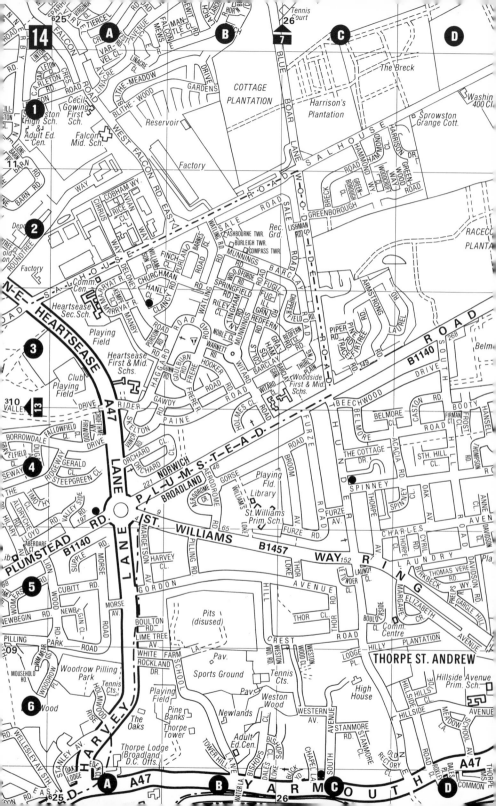

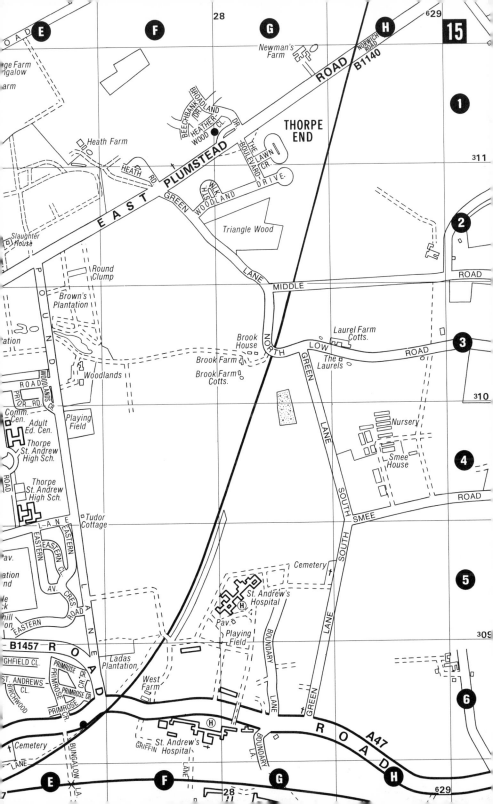

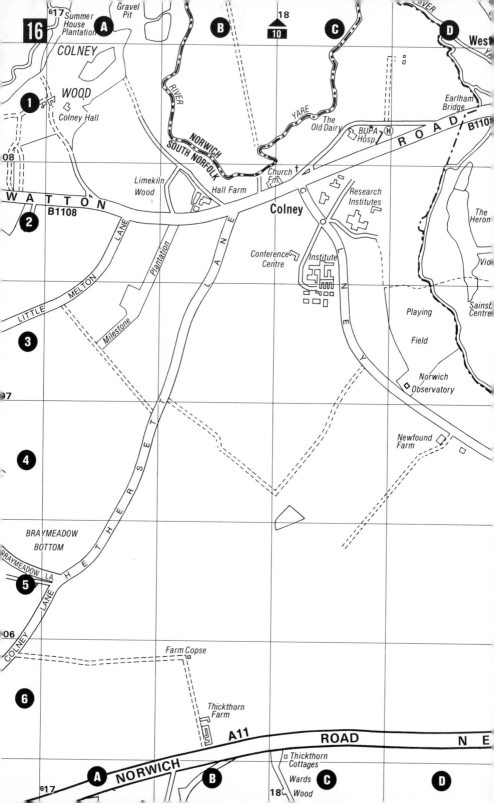

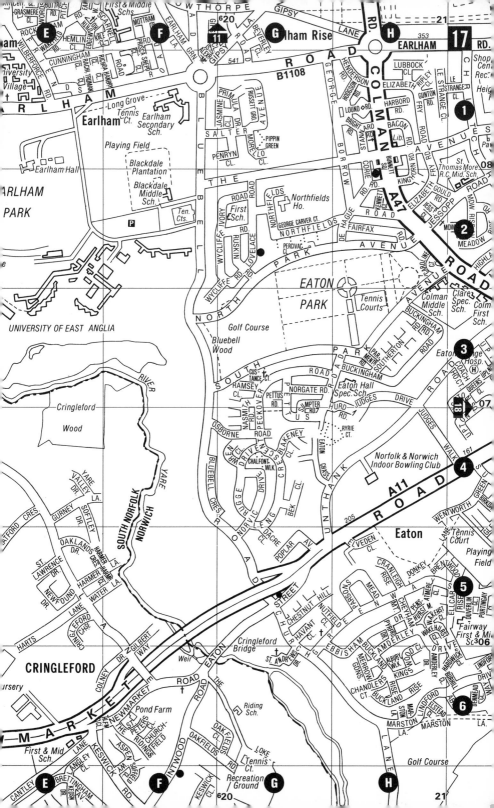

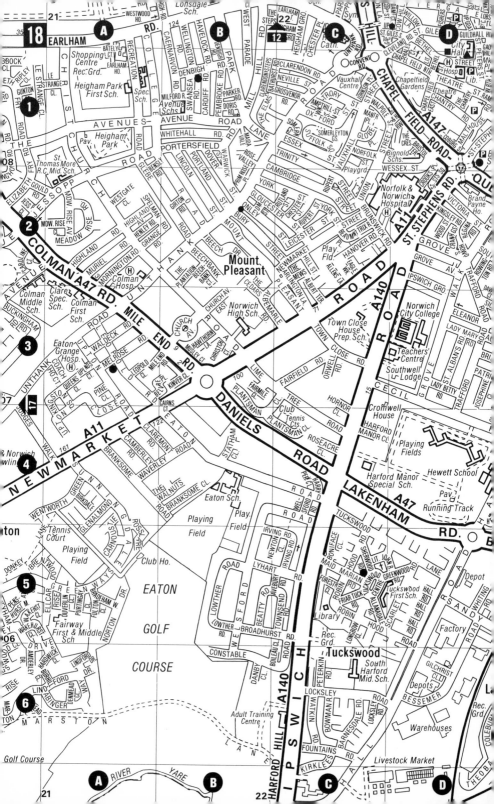

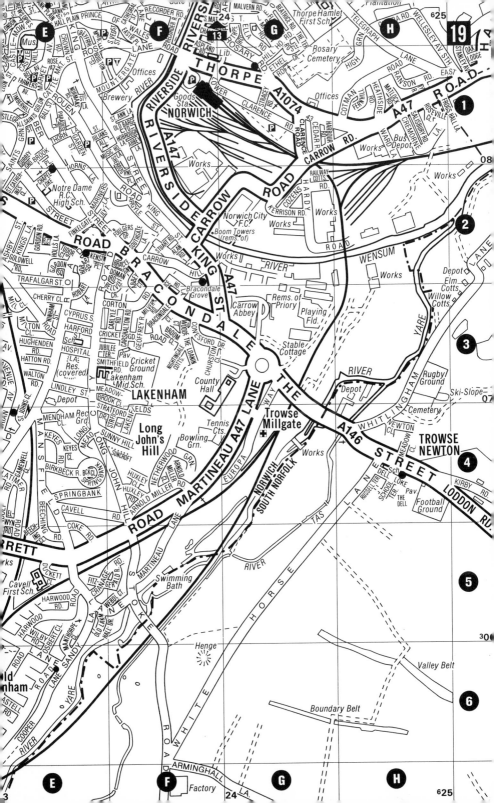

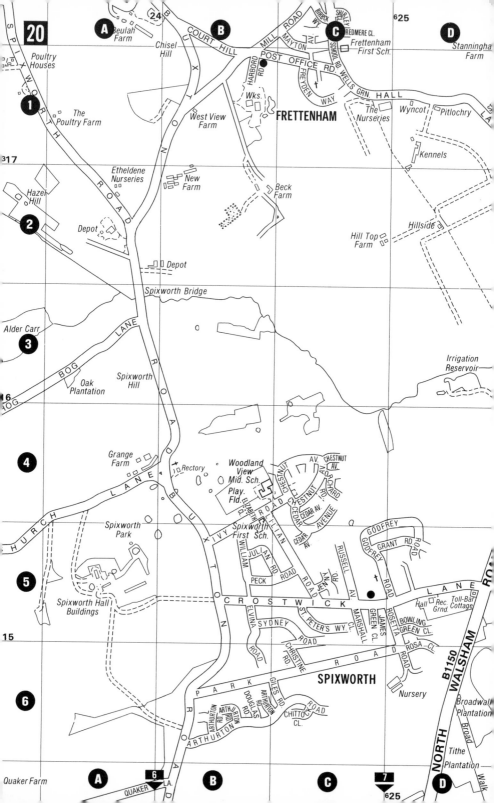

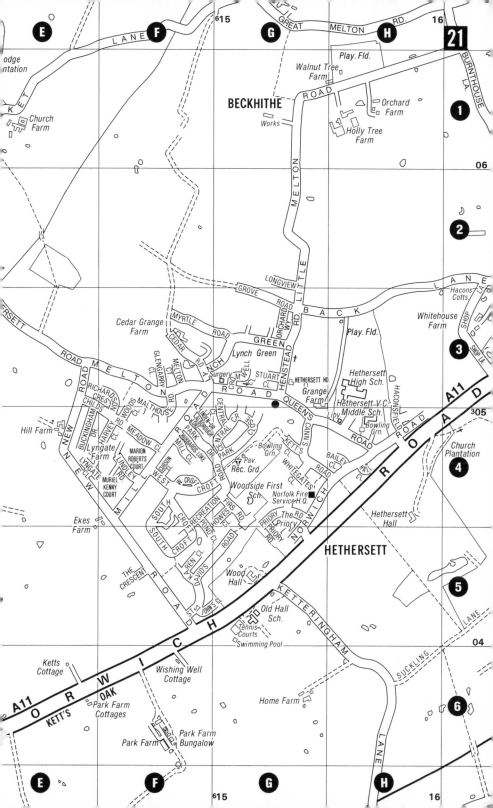

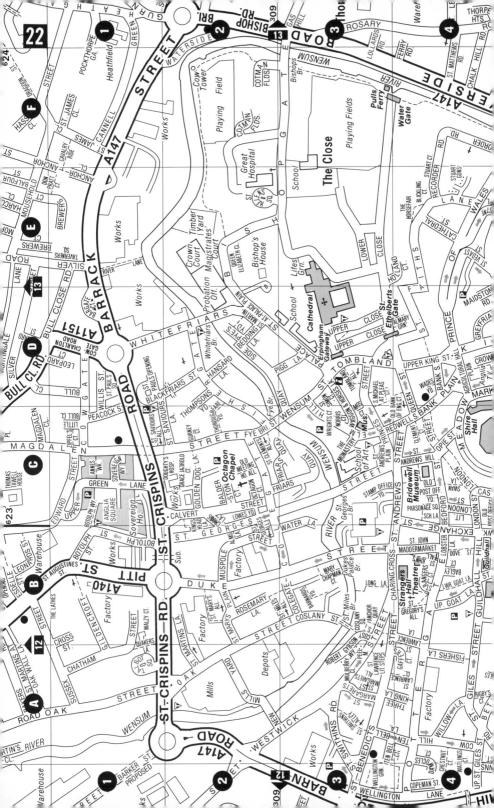

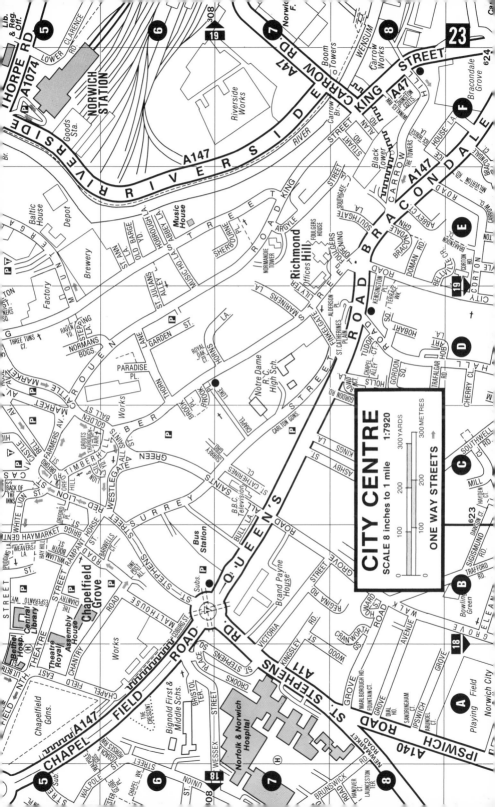

INDEX TO STREETS

HOW TO USE THIS INDEX

1. A strict alphabetical order is followed in which Av., Rd., St., etc. are read in full and as part of the name preceding them; e.g. Ash Gro. follows Ashby St. but precedes Ashtree Rd.
2. Each street is followed by its Postal Code District Number and map reference; e.g. Abbey Ct. NR1—2F 19 is in the Norwich 1 Postal Code District and is to be found in square 2F on page 19.
3. Streets shown in italics refer to those shown only on the large scale map of the City Centre on pages 22 and 23.
N.B. The Postal Code District Numbers given in this index are, in fact, only the first part of the Postcode to each address and are only meant to indicate the Postal Code District in which each street is situated.

ABBREVIATIONS USED IN THIS INDEX

All : Alley	Ct : Court	Lit : Little	Rd : Road
App : Approach	Cres : Crescent	Lwr : Lower	S : South
Arc : Arcade	Dri : Drive	Mans : Mansions	Sq : Square
Av : Avenue	E : East	Mkt : Market	Sta : Station
Bk : Back	Embkmt : Embankment	M : Mews	St : Street
Boulevd : Boulevard	Est : Estate	Mt : Mount	Ter : Terrace
Bri : Bridge	Gdns : Gardens	N : North	Up : Upper
B'way : Broadway	Ga : Gate	NR : Norwich	Vs : Villas
Bldgs : Buildings	Gt : Great	Pal : Palace	Wlk : Walk
Chyd : Churchyard	Grn : Green	Pde : Parade	W : West
Cir : Circus	Gro : Grove	Pk : Park	Yd : Yard
Clo : Close	Ho : House	Pas : Passage	
Comn : Common	Junct : Junction	Pl : Place	
Cotts : Cottages	La : Lane	Prom : Promenade	

INDEX TO STREETS

Abbey Ct. NR1—2F 19
Abbey La. NR1—1F 19
Abbot Rd. NR1—4D 18
Aberdare Ct. NR1—5H 13
Abinger Way. NR4—6A 18
Acacia Rd. NR7—4D 14
Adams Rd. NR7—5C 6
Addey Clo. NR6—5B 6
Adelaide St. NR2—5B 12
(in two parts)
Aerodrome Cres. NR7—4B 14
Aerodrome Rd. NR7—4B 14
Agricultural Hall Plain. NR1
—6E 13
Alan Rd. NR1—2F 19
Albany Rd. NR3—4D 12
Albemarle Rd. NR2—3B 18
Albert Pl. NR1—6G 13
Albert Ter. NR2—2C 18
Alborough Loke. NR9—4F 21
Albury Wlk. NR4—6H 17
Alderson Pl. NR1—8D 23
Aldryche Rd. NR1—4H 13
Alexandra Rd. NR2—6B 12
Alford Gro. NR7—1G 13
Allanadale Rd. NR4—5C 18
Allen's Av. NR7—6C 6
Allens La. NR2—2C 18
Allen's La. NR7—6B 6
Allerton Clo. NR7—1H 13
Allerton Rd. NR7—1H 13
All Saints Grn. NR1—2E 19
All Saints St. NR1—1E 19
Almary Grn. NR1—4D 22
Alma Ter. NR3—4D 12
Alms La. NR3—2B 22
Alnwick Ct. NR5—5B 10
Ambleside Clo. NR5—6E 11
Amderley Dri. NR4—5H 17
Amhirst Clo. NR3—3F 13
Ampthill St. NR2—1C 18
Anchor Clo. NR3—5F 13
Anchor Quay. NR2—3B 22
Anchor St. NR3—4F 13
Angel Rd. NR3—2D 12
Anglia Sq. NR1—5E 13
Anmer Clo. NR3—1F 13
Anna Sewell Dri. NR6—5A 6
Anne Clo. NR7—4D 14
Annes Wlk. NR3—1C 22
Anson Rd. NR6—4F 5
Anthony Dri. NR3—2F 13

Antingham Rd. NR7—3B 14
Appleyard Cres. NR3—1A 12
Apsley Clo. NR5—6H 11
Arcade St. NR2—1E 19
Archer Clo. NR6—4C 6
Arden Gro. NR6—3C 4
Arderon Ct. NR2—5B 12
Ardney Rise. NR3—1D 12
Argyle St. NR1—2F 19
Arlington La. NR2—2C 18
Armes Cres. NR2—4A 12
Armes St. NR2—4A 12
Arminghall Clo. NR3—1C 12
Arminghall La. NR14—6F 19
Armstrong Rd. NR7—3C 14
Arnfield La. NR5—4D 10
Arnold Miller Clo. NR1—4F 19
Arnold Miller Rd. NR1—4F 19
Arthurton Rd. NR10—6B 20
Arundel Ct. NR2—8A 23
Ashbourne Tower. NR7—2B 14
Ashby St. NR1—2E 19
Ash Gro. NR3—2E 13
Ashtree Rd. NR5—2C 10
Aspen Way. NR4—6F 17
Aspland Rd. NR1—6F 13
Astell Rd. NR1—6E 19
Astley Rd. NR5—4B 10
Atkinson Clo. NR5—4A 10
Atmere Clo. NR4—5H 17
Atthill Rd. NR2—5A 12
Aurania Av. NR1—3D 18
Auster Clo. NR6—6G 5
Autumn Dri. NR5—4D 10
Avebury Rd. NR4—5C 18
Avenue Rd. NR2—1B 18
Avenues, The. NR4 & NR2
—1A 18
Avian Way. NR7—2A 14
Avonmouth Rd. NR3—3C 12
Aylesbury Clo. NR2—2E 13
Aylmer Tower. NR3—2A 12
Aylsham Cres. NR3—1C 12
Aylsham Rd. NR3—1B 12
Aylsham Way. NR3—2C 12

Back La. NR9—3G 21
Back of the Inns. NR2—5C 23
Bacon Rd. NR2—1H 17
Bacton Rd. NR3—3B 12
Bagley Ct. NR2—6D 12

Bailey Clo. NR9—4H 21
Bailey Ct. NR2—5C 12
Bakers Rd. NR3—4D 12
Balderston Ct. NR3—5E 13
Baldric Rd. NR8—1D 2
Balfour St. NR3—4F 13
Bank Plain. NR2—6E 13
Bank St. NR3—6E 13
Barclay Grn. NR7—3C 14
Barclay Rd. NR7—3B 14
Barford Rd. NR9—5A 8
Bargate Ct. NR3—5E 13
Barker's La. NR7—5C 6
Barker St. NR2—4C 12
Barnard Rd. NR5—4A 10
Barnes Clo. NR7—2B 14
Barnesdale Rd. NR4—6C 18
Barnham Clo. NR5—5A 10
Barn Rd. NR2—6C 12
Barrack Rd. NR1—5H 13
Barrack St. NR3—5F 13
Barrett Rd. NR1—5E 19
Barwells Ct. NR2—6B 23
Bassingham Rd. NR3—2B 12
Bately Ct. NR2—1A 18
Bateman Clo. NR5—5B 10
Bates Grn. NR5—4E 11
Bathurst Rd. NR2—1B 18
Bawburgh La. NR5—3H 9
Bawburgh Rd. NR9—6E 9
(Bawburgh)
Bawburgh Rd. NR9—3B 8
(Easton)
Bawburgh Rd. NR9—5A 8
(Marlingford)
Beachcroft. NR3—2F 13
Beaconsfield Rd. NR3—4E 13
Beatrice Rd. NR1—6G 13
Beatty Rd. NR4—5B 18
Beaumont Pl. NR2—2C 18
Beaumont Rd. NR5—3D 10
Bedding La. NR3—5E 13
Bedford St. NR2—6E 13
Beech Av. NR8—1A 2
Beechbank. NR2—2B 18
Beechbank Ct. NR2—2B 18
Beechbank Dri. NR13—1F 15
Beech Croft. NR5—3B 10
Beech Dri. NR1—4G 13
Beech Dri. NR2—2B 18
Beech Dri. NR6—6G 5

Beecheno Rd. NR5—5D 10
Beeches Clo. NR6—6B 6
Beeching Clo. NR1—5E 19
Beeching Rd. NR1—4E 19
Beechlands. NR8—1B 2
Beechwood Dri. NR7—3C 14
Beeston La. NR12—2C 6
Bek Clo. NR4—4G 17
Bell Av. NR1—1E 19
Bell Clo. NR6—4D 4
Bellomonte Cres. NR8—2F 3
Bell Rd. NR3—3E 13
Bellville Cres. NR1—2F 19
Belmore Clo. NR7—4C 14
Belmore Rd. NR7—4C 14
Beloe Av. NR5—5C 10
Belsize Rd. NR1—5H 13
Belvedere Pl. NR4—3A 18
Belvoir St. NR2—6B 12
Bendish Way. NR5—5A 10
Bensley Rd. NR2— 2A 18
Berkley Clo. NR6—5E 5
Berners Clo. NR3—3B 12
Berners Ct. NR3—3B 12
Berners St. NR3—3C 12
Bernham Rd. NR6—4C 4
Berrington Rd. NR6—4D 4
Ber St. NR1—1E 19
Bertie Rd. NR3—3C 12
Bessemer Rd. NR4—6D 18
Bethel St. NR2—6D 12
Bevan Clo. NR5—6D 10
Beverley Clo. NR5—6G 11
Beverley Rd. NR5—5G 11
Beverley Way. NR8—2F 3
Bewfield Rd. NR5—4A 10
Bewit Rd. NR7—6F 7
Bidewell Clo. NR8—3H 3
Bignold Rd. NR3—2A 12
Billing Clo. NR6—5B 6
Binyon Gdns. NR8—2D 2
Birbeck Way. NR12—1D 20
Birch Ct. NR7—6F 7
Birchwood. NR7—6E 15
Birkbeck Clo. NR4—4E 19
Birkbeck Rd. NR1—4E 19
Birkbeck Way. NR7—5D 14
Birkdale. NR4—4A 18
Bishop Bri. Rd. NR1—5G 13
Bishopgate. NR3 & NR1—5F 13
Bishops Clo. NR7—6B 14
Bixley Clo. NR5—6F 11

24

Blackfriars St. NR3—5E 13
Blackhorse La. NR3—2F 13
Black Horse Opening. NR3
—2F 13
Black Horse St. NR2—5C 12
Blacksmith's Way. NR6—5A 6
Blackthorn Clo. NR6—6H 5
Blackwell Av. NR7—1G 13
Blakeney Clo. NR4—4G 17
Blakes Ct. NR3—1F 13
Bland St. NR5—6D 10
Blenheim Clo. NR7—5D 6
Blenheim Cres. NR7—6D 6
Blenheim Rd. NR7—5D 6
Blickling Ct. NR1—4E 22
Blickling La. NR6—5G 5
Blithe-Meadow Dri. NR7—1A 14
Blithe-Wood Gdns. NR7—1A 14
Blomfield Rd. NR3—2B 12
Bluebell Cres. NR4—4F 17
Bluebell Rd. NR4—1F 17
Blue Boar La. NR7—5E 7
Blyth Rd. NR3—2D 12
Boileau Clo. NR4—6C 18
Bolingbroke Rd. NR3—1B 12
Bond St. NR2—5A 12
Bone Rd. NR8—2H 3
Boniface Clo. NR4—5C 18
Booty Rd. NR7—3D 14
Borrowdale Dri. NR1—4H 13
Boston St. NR3—2D 12
Botolph St. NR3—5D 12
Botolph Way. NR3—1C 22
Bottom Breck Clo. NR5—2B 10
Boulderside Clo. NR7—5C 14
Boulevard, The. NR13—1G 15
Boulton Rd. NR7—5A 14
Boulton St. NR1—1E 19
Boundary Av. NR6—6E 5
Boundary La. NR7—6G 15
(in two parts)
Boundary Rd. NR6—1H 11
(in two parts)
Bowers Av. NR3—1A 12
Bowers Clo. NR3—2A 12
Bowling Grn. Clo. NR10—5D 20
Bowman Rd. NR4—6C 18
Bowthorpe Cotts. NR5—5D 10
Bowthorpe Rd. NR5 & NR2
—6F 11
Brabazon Rd. NR6—5F 5
Bracey Av. NR5—5B 6
Bracken Av. NR6—6E 5
Bracondale. NR1—2F 19
Bracondale Ct. NR1—3F 19
Bracondale Grn. NR1—2F 19
Bradecroft. NR5—4D 10
Bradeham Way. NR4—5A 18
Bradshaw Rd. NR8—3A 4
Braeford Clo. NR6—2G 11
Braithwait Clo. NR5—4C 10
Brakendon Clo. NR1—8E 23
Bramble Av. NR6—5E 5
Bramfield Clo. NR2—5A 12
Brampton Ct. NR5—4C 10
Brandon Clo. NR6—6C 4
Branford Rd. NR3—3E 13
Branksome Clo. NR4—4B 18
Branksome Rd. NR4—4A 18
Brasier Rd. NR3—2B 12
Brayfield Way. NR6—4B 6
Braymeadow La. NR9—5A 16
Breckland Rd. NR5—3C 10
Breck Rd. NR7—2C 14
Brennewater M. NR5—4C 10
Brentwood. NR4—5H 17
Brereton Clo. NR5—6E 11
Brettingham Av. NR4—6E 17
Brewers Ct. NR3—5F 13
(in two parts)
Breydon Dri. NR8—6C 2
Breydon Dri. N. NR8—5C 2
Breydon Rd. NR7—6B 6
Brian Av. NR1—3D 18

Briar Ct. NR5—5H 11
Brickfield Loke. NR8—5C 2
Brigg St. NR2—1D 18
Bright Rd. NR4—1H 17
Brightwell Rd. NR3—1D 12
Brightys Opening. NR2—5A 12
Bristol Ter. NR2—1D 18
Britannia Ho. NR5—4E 11
Britannia Rd. NR1—4G 13
Broadhurst Rd. NR4—5B 18
Broadland Dri. NR13—1F 15
Brockwell Ct. NR3—2F 13
Brook Pl. NR1—1E 19
Broom Av. NR6—5E 5
Broom Av. NR7—4C 14
Broom Clo. NR1—3F 19
Browne St. NR2—5B 12
Brunswick Rd. NR2—2C 18
Bryony Clo. NR6—5H 5
Buckingham Dri. NR9—4E 21
Buckingham Rd. NR4—3H 17
Buckland Rise. NR4—6H 17
Buck Yd. NR7—6C 14
Bullace Rd. NR5—2B 10
Bullard Rd. NR1—1C 12
Bull Clo. NR3—5E 13
Bull Clo. Rd. NR3—4E 13
Bull La. NR1—2D 18
Bulmer Rd. NR3—2A 12
Bumpstede Ct. NR5—4C 10
Bungalow La. NR7—6E 15
Bunnett Sq. NR4—1H 17
Burges Rd. NR3—3B 12
Burhill Clo. NR4—6A 18
Burleigh Tower. NR7—2B 14
Burma Rd. NR6—5B 6
Burnet Rd. NR3—2H 11
Burnthouse La. NR9—1H 21
Burton Clo. NR6—5G 5
Burton Rd. NR6—5G 5
Bury St. NR2—2B 18
Bush Rd. NR6—3D 4
Bussey Rd. NR6—6H 5
Buttermere Rd. NR5—6E 11
Butts, The. NR5—4B 10
Buxton Rd. NR3—4D 12
Buxton Rd. NR6, NR12 & NR10
—3B 6 to 1B 20
Byfield Ct. NR3—3C 12
Byron Rd. NR8—2D 2

Cadge Clo. NR5—5F 11
Cadge Rd. NR5—5F 11
Caernarvon Rd. NR2—1B 18
Cairns Ct. NR4—3B 18
Caley Clo. NR3—2H 11
(in two parts)
Calthorpe Rd. NR5—5D 10
Calvert St. NR3—5E 13
Camberley Rd. NR4—4A 18
Camborne Clo. NR5—3E 11
Cambridge St. NR2—2C 18
Camp Gro. NR1—6G 13
Campion Ho. NR5—4C 10
Camp Rd. NR8—1C 2
Cannell Grn. NR3—5F 13
Cannerby La. NR7—6D 6
Cann's Rd. NR9—4G 21
Canterbury Pl. NR2—5C 12
Cantley La. NR4—6E 17
Capps Rd. NR3—3E 13
Cardiff Rd. NR2—1B 18
Cardigan Pl. NR2—5C 12
Carleton Clo. NR7—1H 13
Carleton Rd. NR7—1H 13
Carlton Gdns. NR1—7C 23
Carlyle Rd. NR1—3F 19
Carnoustie. NR4—5A 18
Caroline Ct. NR4—2H 17
Carrow Clo. NR1—8E 23
Carrow Hill. NR1—2F 19

Carrow Rd. NR1—2F 19
Carr's Hill Clo. NR8—6G 3
Carshalton Rd. NR1—3F 19
Carterford Dri. NR3—1E 13
Carter Rd. NR8—2H 3
Castle Hill. NR1—1E 19
Castle Meadow. NR1—1E 19
Castle St. NR2—6E 13
Castleton Clo. NR5—8B 10
Caston Rd. NR7—3D 14
Cathedral St. NR1—6F 13
Catherine Wheel Opening.
NR3—4D 12
Cator Rd. NR8—1F 3
Cattle Mkt. St. NR1—1E 19
Catton Chase. NR6—5H 5
Catton Rd. NR3—2D 12
Catton View Ct. NR3—1D 12
Causeway Clo. NR2—5C 12
Cavalry Ride. NR3—1F 22
Cavell Rd. NR1—4E 19
Cecil Gowing Ct. NR7—6D 6
Cecil Rd. NR1—3D 18
Cedar Av. NR10—4C 20
Cedar Rd. NR1—1G 19
Cedar Rd. NR9—3F 21
Cedars, The. NR2—2B 18
Central Clo. NR9—4G 21
Central Cres. NR9—4G 21
Cere Rd. NR7—6E 7
Chalfont Wlk. NR4—4G 17
Chalk Hill Rd. NR1—6F 13
Chamberlin Clo. NR3—2E 13
Chamberlin Rd. NR3—3D 12
Chambers Rd. NR3—1B 12
Chandlers Ct. NR4—6H 17
Chantry Rd. NR2—1D 18
Chantry, The. NR2—1D 18
Chapel All. NR1—8D 23
Chapel Break Rd. NR5—4A 10
Chapel Ct. NR6—5D 4
Chapel Field E. NR2—1D 18
Chapel Field N. NR2—1D 18
Chapel Field Rd. NR2—1D 18
Chapel La. NR7—6C 14
Chapel Loke. NR1—2E 19
Chapel Rd. NR5—2C 10
Chapel Wlk. NR2—6A 23
Charing Cross. NR2—6D 12
Charles Av. NR7—4D 14
Charles Sq. NR2—6C 12
Charles Watling Way. NR5
—4A 10
Charlton Rd. NR3—5E 13
Chartwell Rd. NR7—1F 13
Chartwell Rd NR6 & NR7—1E 13
Chase Clo. NR6—5H 5
Chatham St. NR3—5D 12
Chenery Dri. NR7—5E 7
Cherry Clo. NR1—3E 19
Chester Pl. NR2—6C 12
Chester St. NR2—2C 18
Chestnut Av. NR10—4C 20
Chestnut Clo. NR5—2A 10
Chestnut Ct. NR2—4A 22
Chestnut Hill. NR4—5G 17
Cheyham Mt. NR4—5H 17
Childs Rd. NR9—3E 21
Chipperfield Rd. NR7—3C 14
Chittock Clo. NR10—6C 20
Christchurch Ct. NR2—3B 18
Christchurch Rd. NR2—1A 18
Christine Rd. NR10—6C 20
Christopher Clo. NR1—3D 18
Christopher Rd. NR5—5E 11
Church Av. NR2—3B 18
Church Av. E. NR2—3B 18
Church Clo. NR2—4B 12
Churchfield Rd. NR4—6F 17
Church Grn. NR7—5D 6
Churchill Rd. NR3—4E 13
Church La. NR4—5G 17
Church La. NR7 & NR12—5D 6
Church La. NR9—1A 8

Church La. NR10—5A 20
Churchman Rd. NR7—2A 14
Church St. NR6—5A 6
Church St. NR8—6E 9
Church View Clo. NR7—5D 6
Church View Ct. NR7—5D 6
Churston Clo. NR4—3F 19
Cintra Rd. NR1—6H 13
Cirrus Way. NR7—2A 14
City Rd. NR1—3E 19
City View Rd. NR6—6E 5
Civic Gdns. NR3—1A 12
Clabon First Clo. NR3—1E 13
Clabon Rd. NR3—2F 13
Clabon Second Clo. NR3—1F 13
Clabon Third Clo. NR3—1F 13
Clancy Rd. NR7—3A 14
Clare Clo. NR3—3E 13
Claremont Rd. NR1—1G 19
Clarence Rd. NR1—1G 19
Clarendon Rd. NR2—1C 18
Clarendon Steps. NR2—1B 18
Clarke Rd. NR3—4E 13
Clarkson Rd. NR5—5E 11
Clement Ct. NR3—4C 22
Cleveland Rd. NR2—6D 12
Clifton Clo. NR2—5C 12
Clifton St. NR2—5B 12
Clovelly Dri. NR6—2G 11
Clover Hill Rd. NR5—4C 10
Clover Rd. NR7—1F 13
Coach & Horses Row. NR2
—1D 18
Coach Ho. Ct. NR4—3A 18
Cobham Way. NR2—2A 14
Coburg St. NR2—1D 18
Coke Rd. NR1—5E 19
Coldershaw Rd. NR6—6F 5
Coleburn Rd. NR1—6D 18
Colegate. NR3—6D 12
(in two parts)
Coleridge Clo. NR8—2D 2
Colindeep La. NR7—6C 6
Colkett Dri. NR6—1E 13
College Rd. NR2—1A 18
Collins Ct. NR3—2D 12
Colls Rd. NR7—3B 14
Colman Rd. NR4—1H 17
Colney Dri. NR4—6F 17
Colney La. NR4—2C 16
Colney La. NR9—6A 16
Common La. NR7—6D 14
Compass Tower. NR7—2B 14
Concorde Rd. NR6—6G 5
Conesford Dri. NR1—3F 19
Coniston Clo. NR5—6E 11
Connaught Rd. NR2—6B 12
Constable Rd. NR4—6B 18
Constitution Hill. NR3 & NR6
—2E 13
Constitution Opening. NR3
—2E 13
Convent Rd. NR2—1C 18
Cooper La. NR1—6E 19
Copeman St. NR2—6C 12
Coppice Av. NR6—5C 4
Corbet Av. NR7—2H 13
Corie Rd. NR4—2H 17
Cornwallis St. NR5—5C 10
Coronation Clo. NR6—6E 5
Coronation Rd. NR6—1A 12
Corton Ho. NR1—8E 23
Corton Rd. NR1—3F 19
Coslany Sq. NR2—4B 22
Coslany St. NR3—6D 12
Costessey La. NR8—4E 3
Costessey Rd. NR8—2C 2
Cotman Fields. NR1—5F 13
Cotman Rd. NR1—1H 19
Cottage Dri., The. NR7—4C 14
Cottinghams Dri. NR6—4C 4
Coughtrey Clo. NR7—6D 6
Courtenay Clo. NR5—4B 10
Court Hill. NR12—1B 20

Cowgate. NR3—5E 13
Cow Hill. NR2—6D 12
Cozens Hardy Rd. NR7—5D 6
Cozens Rd. NR1—2G 19
Cranage Rd. NR1—5E 19
Cranleigh Rise. NR4—5H 17
Cranworth Gdns. NR1—2D 18
Creance Rd. NR7—6E 7
Cremorne La. NR1—1H 19
Crescent, The. NR2—1D 18
Crescent, The. NR9—5F 21
Cressener Clo. NR6—5C 4
Cresswell Clo. NR5—6D 10
Cricket Ground Rd. NR1—3F 19
Cringleford Chase. NR4—5E 17
Croftholme Way. NR1—4A 14
Crofts, The. NR5—5B 10
Croft, The. NR8—6F 3
Crome Rd. NR3—3F 13
Cromer Rd. NR6—4E 5
  (in two parts)
Cromwell Clo. NR9—3G 21
Cromwell Rd. NR7—1H 13
Crooks Pl. NR2—2D 18
Cross La. NR3—2C 22
Cross St. NR3—5D 12
Crostwick La. NR10—5B 20
Crown Rd. NR1—6E 13
Crown Rd. NR3—5D 10
Crummock Rd. NR5—6E 11
Cubitt Rd. NR1—5A 14
Cunningham Rd. NR5—1E 17
Curson Rd. NR9—4F 21
Curtis Rd. NR6—6F 5
Custance Ct. NR4—3G 17
Cuthbert Clo. NR7—6D 6
Cutler Way. NR5—4A 10
Cypress Clo. NR8—2E 3
Cyprus St. NR1—3E 19
Cyril Rd. NR7—5D 14

Dacre Clo. NR4—5G 17
Dakin Rd. NR3—3D 12
Dales Loke. NR7—6B 14
Dales Pl. NR7—6D 14
Damocles Ct. NR2—6D 12
Danby Clo. NR4—6B 18
Daniels Rd. NR4—4B 18
Darrell Pl. NR5—5F 11
Davey Pl. NR2—5C 23
Davidson Clo. NR7—5D 14
Davidson Rd. NR7—5D 14
Dawson Ct. NR1—3D 18
De Caux Rd. NR3—3E 13
De Hague Rd. NR4—2H 17
Delane Rd. NR8—3A 4
Dell Cres. NR5—5G 11
Dell Loke. NR14—4H 19
Dell, The. NR14—4H 19
Deloney Rd. NR7—2A 14
Delta Clo. NR6—6G 5
Denbigh Ho. NR2—1B 18
Denbigh Rd. NR2—1B 18
Denmark Opening. NR3—3E 13
Denmark Rd. NR3—3E 13
Denmead Rd. NR4—6A 18
Dennis Rd. NR6—3D 4
Denton Rd. NR3—1F 13
Derby St. NR2—5C 12
Dereham Rd. NR2—5H 11
Dereham Rd. NR9 & NR5—2A 3
Desmond Dri. NR6—4B 6
Devon Av. NR6—6C 4
Devonshire St. NR2—5C 12
Dial Ho. NR1—8A 23
Diamond Rd. NR6—5F 5
Dibden Rd. NR3—4F 13
Distillery Sq. NR2—6C 12
Dixon Rd. NR7—6C 6
Dixon's Fold. NR6—6B 6
Dog La. NR9—1A 8
Dogwood Rd. NR6—6H 5
Dolphin Gro. NR2—4B 12

Dolphin Path. NR2 & NR3—4C 12
Doman Rd. NR1—2F 19
Donchurch Clo. NR5—5C 10
Donkey La. NR4—5H 17
Don Pratt Ct. NR3—1E 22
Doris Rd. NR2—1B 18
Douglas Clo. NR6—3H 5
Douglas Haig Rd. NR5—6F 11
Douglas Rd. NR10—6B 20
Douro Pl. NR2—6C 12
Dovedales. NR6—6B 6
Dovedales Ct. NR6—6B 6
Dover St. NR2—1B 18
Dove St. NR2—4B 22
Dowding Rd. NR6—4H 5
Dowson Rd. NR3—3B 12
Dragoon Rd. NR3—4F 13
Draper Way. NR5—4A 10
Drayton Gro. NR8—2F 3
Drayton High Rd. NR8 & NR6
                        —3G 3
Drayton Rd. NR3—2H 11
Drayton Wood Rd. NR6—4B 4
Drive, The. NR5—3D 10
Drury Clo. NR5—4D 10
Dryden Rd. NR8—2D 2
Duckett Clo. NR1—5E 19
Duff Rd. NR3—2D 12
Dugard Av. NR4—4H 13
Duke St. NR3—5D 12
Dunston Cotts. NR1—8F 23
Dunwood Dri. NR6—3B 6
Durham St. NR2—2B 18
Duverlin Clo. NR4—5A 18

Eade Rd. NR3—4D 12
Eagle Wlk. NR2—2C 18
Earlham Ct. NR2—6C 12
Earlham Grn. La. NR5
                —5B to 6F 11
Earlham Gro. NR5—6F 11
Earlham Ho. NR5—1A 18
Earlham Rd. NR4 & NR2—1E 17
Earlham W. Centre. NR5—6E 11
Eastbourne Pl. NR1—6F 13
Eastern Av. NR7—5E 15
Eastern Clo. NR7—5E 15
Eastern Cres. NR7—5E 15
Eastern Rd. NR7—5E 15
Eastfield. NR8—2D 2
E. Hills Rd. NR5—3A 10
Easton Rd. NR9—5A 8
Eastwood M. NR6—1E 13
Eaton Chase. NR4—4G 17
Eaton Rd. NR4—4B 18
Eaton St. NR4—6F 17
Ebbisham Dri. NR4—6H 17
Ecton Wlk. NR6—5B 6
Eden Clo. NR7—6A 14
Edgefield Clo. NR6—3B 6
Edgeworth Rd. NR5—6E 11
Edinburgh Rd. NR2—6B 12
Edmund Bacon Ct. NR3—3D 12
Edward Gambling Ct. NR2
                        —4B 12
Edwards Rd. NR7—5C 6
Edward St. NR3—4D 12
Eleanor Rd. NR1—3D 18
Elizabeth Av. NR7—5D 14
Elizabeth Clo. NR7—5D 6
Elizabeth Rd. NR10—4B 20
Elizabeth Fry Rd. NR2—1H 17
Ella Rd. NR1—6G 13
Ellcar Rise. NR4—5A 18
Elm Clo. NR5—2B 10
Elmdon Ct. NR1—6G 13
Elm Gro. La. NR3—2D 12
Elm Hill. NR3—6E 13
Elms, The. NR2—1B 18
Elstead Clo. NR4—6H 17
Elveden Clo. NR4—5H 17
Elvina Rd. NR10—5B 20
Elwyn Rd. NR1—4E 19

Ely St. NR2—5C 12
Embry Clo. NR6—4H 5
Enfield Rd. NR5—6E 11
English Rd. NR6—6A 6
Esdelle St. NR3—4D 12
Esperanto Way. NR2—5B 23
Essex St. NR2—1C 18
Ethel Rd. NR1—1G 19
Europa Way. NR1—4G 19
Eustace Rd. NR3—1A 12
Eversley Rd. NR6—6F 5
Everson Rd. NR5—3E 11
Exchange St. NR2—6D 12
Exeter St. NR2—5C 12

Fairfax Rd. NR4—2H 17
Fairfield Rd. NR2—3C 18
Fairmile Clo. NR2—3B 18
Fairstead Ct. NR7—1G 13
Fairstead Rd. NR7—1G 13
Fairview Clo. NR8—3G 3
Fairways. NR6—5B 4
Fakenham Rd. NR8—1C 2
Falcon M. NR7—6E 7
Falcon Rd. E. NR7—1A 14
Falcon Rd. W. NR7—6D 6
Falkland Clo. NR6—5B 4
Fallowfield Clo. NR1—4A 14
Farmers Av. NR1—1E 19
Farmland Rd. NR5—2B 10
Farrow Rd. NR5—6H 11
Fastolf Clo. NR6—5C 4
Fenn Cres. NR3—3B 12
Ferndale Clo. NR6—6C 4
Fernhill Rd. NR1—1H 19
Ferry Rd. NR1—6F 13
Fiddle Wood Rd. NR6—6H 5
Fieldview. NR6—4D 4
Fifers La. NR6—4F 5
Finch Clo. NR7—3C 14
Finkelgate. NR1—2E 19
Firman Ct. NR7—4D 14
Firs Rd. NR6—4D 4
Firs Rd. NR9—4G 21
Firtree Rd. NR7—3C 14
Firwood Clo. NR1—4A 14
Fishergate. NR3—5E 13
Fisher's Clo. NR5—3A 10
Fishers La. NR2—6D 12
Fitzgerald Rd. NR1—5E 19
Fitzhenry M. NR5—4D 10
Fleet Rd. NR8—4B 2
Florence Rd. NR1—6G 13
Folgate Clo. NR8—5F 3
Folgate La. NR8—5F 3
Folwell Rd. NR5—3A 10
Forester Clo. NR4—5C 18
Foster Rd. NR3—1D 12
Foulgers Ho. NR1—7E 23
Foulgers Opening. NR1—2F 19
Fountain Ct. NR1—8A 23
Fountains Rd. NR4—6C 18
Fowell Clo. NR5—6D 10
Foxburrow Rd. NR7—5C 6
Foxcote Clo. NR6—3C 4
Foxley Clo. NR5—6F 11
Frances Ct. NR2—6B 12
Francis Way. NR5—3A 10
Frenbury Est. NR6—1H 11
Frensham Rd. NR3—3H 11
Frere Rd. NR7—3B 14
Freshfield Clo. NR5—5E 11
Freyden Way. NR12—1C 20
Friars Quay. NR3—6E 13
Friar Tuck Rd. NR4—5C 18
Friends Rd. NR5—1E 17
Frogs Hall La. NR1—1H 19
Frost Clo. NR7—4D 14
Fugill Grn. NR7—3B 14
Fugill Rd. NR7—2B 14
Fulton Clo. NR4—5A 18
Furze Av. NR7—4C 14

Furze Rd. NR7—4C 14
Fye Bri. St. NR3—5E 13

Gaffers Ct. NR2—4A 22
Gage Rd. NR7—6E 7
Galley Hill. NR3—2A 12
Gamewell Clo. NR1—4E 19
Gaol Hill. NR2—6D 12
Garden Pl. NR3—4E 13
Garden St. NR1—1E 19
Gargle Hill. NR7—5D 14
Garrick Grn. NR6—5A 6
Gas Hill. NR1—6G 13
Gateley Gdns. NR3—1C 12.
Gawdy Rd. NR7—3B 14
Gayton Wlk. NR6—4B 6
Gentleman's Wlk. NR2—1D 18
Gentry Pl. NR5—4E 11
Geoffrey Rd. NR1—3F 19
George Borrow Rd. NR4—1G 17
George Carver Ct. NR4—2G 17
George Clo. NR8—2H 3
George Dri. NR8—3H 3
George Hill. NR6—6A 6
George Pope Clo. NR3—2C 12
George Pope Rd. NR3—2C 12
Gerald Clo. NR1—4A 14
Gertrude Rd. NR3—3F 13
Gilbard Rd. NR5—5E 11
Gilbert Way. NR4—5F 17
Gilchrist Clo. NR4—6D 18
Gildencroft. NR3—5D 12
Giles Rd. NR10—6C 20
Gilman Rd. NR3—3F 13
Gipsy Clo. NR5—6F 11
Gipsy La. NR5—6G 11
Girton Rd. NR2—2B 18
Glade, The. NR8—6F 3
Gladstone St. NR2—6B 12
Glebe Clo. NR8—1F 3
Glebe Rd. NR2—2A 18
Glenalmond. NR4—4A 18
Glenburn Av. NR7—1G 13
Glenburn Clo. NR7—1G 13
Glenda Clo. NR3—5D 10
Glenda Ct. NR5—2E 11
Glenda Cres. NR5—2E 11
Glenda Rd. NR5—3E 11
Glengarry Clo. NR9—3F 21
Glenmore Gdns. NR3—3B 12
Globe Pl. NR2—1C 18
Gloucester St. NR2—2B 18
Godfrey Rd. NR10—5C 20
Godric Pl. NR2—6H 11
Golden Ball St. NR1—1E 19
Golden Dog La. NR3—5E 13
Golding Pl. NR2—6C 12
Goldsmith St. NR2—5C 12
Goldwell Rd. NR1—2E 19
Goodhale Rd. NR5—5D 10
Goodman Sq. NR2—5D 12
Gordon Av. NR7—5A 14
Gordon Rd. NR1—2E 19
Gordon Sq. NR1—2E 19
Gorse Av. NR6—5E 5
Gorse Rd. NR7—4B 14
Goulburn Rd. NR7—3B 14
Gould Rd. NR2—2H 17
Gowing Clo. NR6—3D 4
Gowing Ct. NR3—1B 12
Gowing Rd. NR6—4D 4
Grace Jarrold Ct. NR3—2C 22
Graham Sq. NR1—3D 18
Grange Clo. NR6—6A 6
Grange Rd. NR2—2A 18
Grant Rd. NR10—5D 20
Grant St. NR2—5A 12
Grapes Hill. NR2—6C 12
Grasmere Clo. NR5—6E 11
Gravelfield Clo. NR1—4H 13
Gt. Melton Rd. NR9—1G 21
Greenborough Clo. NR7—2C 14
Greenborough Rd. NR7—2C 14

26

Green Clo. NR5—3A 10
Green Hills Clo. NR8—1B 10
Green Hills Rd. NR3—4D 12
Green La. N. NR13—2F 15
Green La. S. NR13 & NR7—3G 15
Greenways. NR4—5H 17
Greenwood Rd. NR4—5D 18
Greenwood Way. NR7—2D 14
Gresham Rd. NR3—2A 12
Greyfriars Clo. NR6—5A 6
Greyfriars Rd. NR1—6E 13
Greyhound Opening. NR2—5C 12
Griffin La. NR7—6F 13
Gristock Pl. NR5—4E 11
Grosvenor Rd. NR2—1C 18
Grouts Thoroughfare. NR1
                    —5C 23
Grove Av. NR1—2D 18
Grove Av. NR5—3B 10
Grovedale Clo. NR5—3C 10
Grove Rd. NR1—2D 18
Grove Rd. NR9—3G 21
Grove, The. NR3—1D 12
Grove Wlk. NR1—3D 18
Guardian Rd. NR5—5H 11
Guelph Rd. NR1—6G 13
Guernsey Rd. NR3—4E 13
Guildhall Hill. NR2—6D 12
Gunn Rd. NR7—3B 14
Gunns Ct. NR2—6C 12
Gunton La. NR5—2D 10
  (in two parts)
Gunton Rd. NR2—1H 17
Gurney Ct. NR3—2C 22
Gurney Ct. NR5—4C 10
Gurney La. NR4—4E 17
Gurney Rd. NR1—5G 13
Gurney Rd. NR5—3C 10

Haconsfield. NR9—3H 21
Haig Clo. NR5—6F 11
Halcolme Ct. NR3—3E 13
Halden Av. NR6—4D 4
Hales Ct. NR2—1D 18
Half Mile Clo. NR3—3B 12
Half Mile Rd. NR3—3B 12
Hall Clo. NR9—4H 21
Hall Dri. NR5—1H 9
Hall Farm Pl. NR9—6F 9
Hall La. NR8—2G 3
Hall Rd. NR4 & NR1—6C 18
Hall Rd. NR5—2C 10
Hall Rd. NR9—3B 8
Hamlin Ct. NR3—2C 12
Hammond Clo. NR7—1C 14
Hammond Way. NR7—1C 14
Hamond Rd. NR6—5B 4
Hanbury Clo. NR5—1F 17
Hanly Clo. NR7—3A 14
Hanover Ct. NR2—8A 23
Hanover Rd. NR2—2C 18
Hansard Clo. NR3—3B 12
Hansard La. NR3—5E 13
Hansard Rd. NR3—3B 12
Hansell Rd. NR7—4D 14
Harbord Rd. NR4—1H 17
Harbord Rd. NR12—1B 20
Harbour Rd. NR1—1G 19
Harcourt Clo. NR3—4F 13
Hardwick Clo. NR4—6A 18
Hardy Rd. NR1—2G 19
Harford Hill. NR4—6C 18
Harford Mnr. Clo. NR2—4C 18
Harford St. NR1—3E 19
Harlington Av. NR6—6E 5
Harmer Clo. NR4—5F 17
Harmer Cres. NR4—5E 17
Harmer La. NR4—5E 17
Harmer Rd. NR3—1C 12
Harpsfield. NR5—4A 10
Harrison Dri. NR7—1C 14

Harry Barber Clo. NR5—4C 10
Harry Perry Clo. NR4—4C 18
Harsnett Clo. NR5—4B 10
Harts La. NR4—5E 17
Harts La. NR9—5E 9
Harvey Clo. NR7—5A 14
Harvey Clo. NR9—4F 21
Harvey La. NR7—6A 14
Harwood Rd. NR1—5E 19
Haslips Clo. NR2—5C 12
Hassett Clo. NR3—4F 13
Hastings Av. NR6—6E 5
Hatton Rd. NR1—3E 19
Hauteyn Ct. NR3—2C 12
Havant Clo. NR4—5G 17
Havelock Rd. NR2—3B 12
Havers Rd. NR3—3B 12
Hawthorne Av. NR6—5E 5
Hawthorn La. NR2—3B 18
Hawthorn Rd. NR5—2C 10
Hawthorn Row. NR2—5B 12
Hayden Ct. NR1—3E 19
Hay Hill. NR2—5B 23
Haymarket. NR2—1D 18
Hazel Rd. NR5—2B 10
Heartsease La. NR7—3A 14
Heath Clo. NR6—4F 5
Heath Cres. NR6—5E 5
Heather Av. NR6—6E 5
Heatherwood Clo. NR13—1F 15
Heathgate. NR3—5G 13
Heath Rd. NR3—4D 12
Heath Rd. NR13—2F 15
Heathside Rd. NR1—1H 19
Hedgerows, The. NR5—5C 10
Heigham Gro. NR2—6C 12
Heigham Rd. NR2—6B 12
Heigham St. NR2—4B 12
Heigham Watering. NR2—4B 12
Helena Rd. NR2—6B 12
Helford St. NR2—4B 12
Hellesdon Clo. NR6—4F 11
Hellesdon Hall Rd. NR3—2H 11
Hellesdon Hall Rd. NR6—2G 11
Hellesdon M. NR6—2F 11
Hellesdon Mill La. NR6—3F 11
Hellesdon Pk. Industrial Est.
                    NR6—2G 11
Hellesdon Pk. Rd. NR6—1G 11
Hellesdon Rd. NR6—4F 11
Hemlin Clo. NR5—6E 11
Hemmings Clo. NR5—5B 10
Henderson Rd. NR4—1H 17
Hendon Clo. NR5—3D 10
Henley Rd. NR2—2A 18
Henstead Rd. NR9—3G 21
Herbert Nursery Clo. NR8—3A 4
Hercules Clo. NR6—6D 4
Hercules Rd. NR6—6D 4
Herrick Rd. NR8—2E 3
Hethersett La. NR9 & NR4
                    —5A 16
Hethersett Rd. NR9—3E 21
Hewett Yd. NR1—4D 18
Higham Clo. NR1—3E 19
Highfield Clo. NR7—6E 15
Highfield Rd. NR8—1F 3
High Grn. NR1—1H 19
Highland Av. NR2—2A 18
Highland Rd. NR2—2A 18
Highland Rd. NR8—2D 2
Highlands. NR8—6F 3
Highlow Rd. NR5—3C 10
Hilary Av. NR1—5H 13
Hill Crest Rd. NR7—5B 14
Hill Farm Clo. NR4—6F 17
Hill Ho. Rd. NR1—1G 19
Hillmead. NR3—1D 12
Hill Rd. NR5—2C 10
Hillside Av. NR7—6D 14
Hillside Clo. NR7—6D 14
Hillside Rd. NR7—6D 14
Hill St. NR2—2C 18
Hillvue Clo. NR5—2C 10

Hilly Plantation. NR7—5C 14
Hobart La. NR1—3E 19
Hobart Sq. NR1—2E 19
Hobrough La. NR1—1F 19
Hockering La. NR5—6F 9
Hodgson Rd. NR4—1H 17
Hog Bog La. NR10—3A 20
Holland Ct. NR1—6F 13
Holls La. NR1—2E 19
Holly Bank. NR7—2G 13
Holly Dri. NR2—5A 12
Holmes Clo. NR7—4B 14
Holmwood Rise. NR7—6A 14
Holt Rd. NR10 & NR6—1C 4
Holworthy Rd. NR5—4D 10
Home St. NR2—4C 12
Honey Clo. NR1—5H 13
Hooker Rd. NR7—3B 14
.Hooper La. NR3—2F 13
Hornbeam Clo. NR7—6F 7
Horning Clo. NR5—5F 11
Hornor Clo. NR2—3C 18
Horns La. NR1—2E 19
Horsefair, The. NR1—4E 22
Horseshoe Clo. NR5—3A 10
Horsford St. NR2—4B 12
Hospital La. NR1—3E 19
Hospital La. NR6—1F 11
Hotblack Rd. NR2—5A 12
Houghton Clo. NR5—4D 10
Howard M. NR3—3E 13
Howard St. NR1—2D 18
Howell Rd. NR8—4A 4
Howes Clo. NR9—4G 21
Howlett Dri. NR5—4C 10
Hubbards Loke. NR9—4F 21
Hudson Way. NR5—5A 10
Hughenden Rd. NR1—3E 19
Humbleyard. NR5—5C 10
Hunter Rd. NR3—1C 12
Huntingfield. NR5—3B 10
Hurd Rd. NR4—3H 17
Hurn Rd. NR8—3A 4
Hurricane Way. NR6—4G 5
Hutchinson Clo. NR5—6F 11
Huxley Clo. NR1—4F 19
Huxley Rd. NR1—4F 19

Ice Ho. La. NR1—2F 19
Ilex Ct. NR7—6F 7
Impala Clo. NR6—4C 6
Ingleby Rd. NR1—1H 19
Inman Rd. NR7—6F 7
Intwood Rd. NR4—6F 17
Ipswich Gro. NR2—2D 18
Ipswich Rd. NR4 & NR2—6C 18
Irstead Rd. NR5—6G 11
Irving Rd. NR4—5C 18
Ives Rd. NR6—5H 5
Ivory Rd. NR4—2G 17
Ivy Rd. NR10—5B 20

James Alexander M. NR5—1F 17
James Green Clo. NR10—5C 20
Jamieson Pl. NR5—4E 11
Jarrold Way. NR5—4B 10
Jasmine Clo. NR4—1G 17
Javelin Rd. NR6—3G 5
Jenny Rd. NR10—5C 20
Jerningham Rd. NR5—3C 10
Jessop Clo. NR2—2H 17
Jessop Rd. NR2—2H 17
Jewson Rd. NR3—2C 12
Jex Av. NR5—4F 11
Jex La. NR5—4F 11
Jex Rd. NR5—4F 11
Joe Ellis Ct. NR5—4D 10
John Howes Clo. NR9—2A 8
Johnson Pl. NR2—1C 18
Jordans Clo. NR5—6D 10
Josephine Clo. NR1—3D 18
Jubilee Rd. NR7—6C 6

Jubilee Ter. NR1—3F 19
Judges Dri. NR4—3H 17
Judges Wlk. NR4—4H 17
Julian Rd. NR10—5B 20
Junction Rd. NR3—3C 12
Jupiter Rd. NR6—6G 5

Kabin Rd. NR5—2D 10
Karen Clo. NR9—5F 21
Keable Clo. NR5—6E 11
Keats Rd. NR8—2D 2
Kedelston Dri. NR4—6E 17
Kempe Clo. NR7—3A 14
Kennedy Clo. NR9—2A 8
Kennett Clo. NR4—2H 17
Kensington Pl. NR1—2E 19
Kered Clo. NR6—4D 4
Kered Rd. NR6—4D 4
Kerridges, The. NR5—3B 10
Kerrison Rd. NR1—2G 19
Kerville St. NR5—5C 10
Kestrel Rd. NR7—6E 7
Keswick Clo. NR4—6F 17
Keswick Rd. NR4—6F 17
Keswick Rd. NR7—6C 6
Ketteringham La. NR9—5G 21
Kett's Clo. NR9—4G 21
Kett's Hill. NR1—5G 13
Kett's Oak. NR9—6E 21
Keyes Clo. NR1—4E 19
Keyes Rd. NR1—4E 19
Kiln Clo. NR6—3A 6
Kinghorn Rd. NR2—2H 17
Kings Head La. NR3—2B 22
Kings La. NR1—2E 19
Kingsley Rd. NR1—4F 19
Kingston Sq. NR4—3A 18
King St. NR1—6E 13 to 3F 19
Kingsway. NR2—4C 12
Kingswood Clo. NR4—6H 17
Kinsale Av. NR6—5C 4
Kinver Av. NR4—3B 18
Kirby Rd. NR14—4H 17
Kirklees. NR4—6C 18
Kirkpatrick Rd. NR3—3B 12
Knights Rd. NR3—3B 12
Knowland Gro. NR5—4E 11
Knowsley Rd. NR3—4E 13
Knox Av. NR1—4H 13
Knox Clo. NR1—4H 13
Knox Rd. NR1—5H 13

Laburnum Av. NR8—1B 2
Lacey Rd. NR8—1D 2
Ladbroke Pl. NR1—5G 13
Lady Betty Rd. NR1—3D 18
Lady Mary Rd. NR1—3D 18
Ladysmith Rd. NR3—3F 13
Lakenfields. NR1—4F 19
Lakenham Rd. NR4—4C 18
Lambert Rd. NR7—1G 13
Lancaster Clo. NR6—4H 5
Lane, The. NR3—2B 12
Langham Pl. NR1—2D 18
Langley Clo. NR4—6E 17
Langton Clo. NR5—5D 10
Larch Clo. NR7—6F 7
Larkman La. NR5—6E 11
Lathes, The. NR3—1B 22
Latimer Rd. NR1—4E 19
Launceston Ter. NR2—8A 23
Laundry Clo. NR7—5C 14
Laundry La. NR7—6F 7
  (Sprowston)
Laundry La. NR7—5D 14
  (Thorpe St Andrew)
Laurel Rd. NR7—3D 14
Lavengro Rd. NR3—4F 13
Lawn Cres. NR13—1G 15
Lawson Rd. NR3—3E 13
Layer Clo. NR5—5B 10

Layton Clo. NR8—3H 3
Leas Ct. NR6—4F 11
Leewood Cres. NR5—3E 11
Lefroy Rd. NR3—1A 12
Leicester St. NR2—2C 18
Leng Cres. NR4—4G 17
Leonards St. NR3—4D 12
Leopard Ct. NR3—5E 13
Leopold Clo. NR4—3A 18
Leopold Rd. NR4—3A 18
Le Strange Clo. NR2—1H 17
Le Tunder Clo. NR7—5C 14
Leveson Rd. NR7—1H 13
Leyham Ct. NR5—4C 10
Liberator Rd. NR6—4G 5
Libra Ct. NR7—6E 7
Lilburne Av. NR3—2D 12
Lilian Clo. NR6—6F 5
Lilian Rd. NR10—5C 20
Lily Ter. NR1—2E 19
Lime Tree Av. NR7—5A 14
Lime Tree Av. NR8—6F 3
Lime Tree Rd. NR2—3B 18
Linacre Av. NR7—1A 14
Linacre Clo. NR7—1A 14
Linalls Dri. NR8—6C 2
Lincoln St. NR2—1B 18
Linden Dri. NR9—4F 21
Linden Rd. NR5—3E 11
Lindford Dri. NR4—6H 17
Lindley Rd. NR9—4F 21
Lindley St. NR1—3E 19
Lindsay Rd. NR7—6E 7
Links Av. NR6—5D 4
Links Clo. NR6—5D 4
Lintock Rd. NR3—1D 12
Linton Clo. NR7—1H 13
Linton Cres. NR7—6D 6
Lion & Castle Yd. NR1—5C 23
Lion Wood Rd. NR1—5A 14
Lishman Rd. NR7—2C 14
Lisle Rd. NR5—4B 10
Lit. Armes St. NR2—4A 12
Lit. Bethel St. NR2—1D 18
Lit. Bull Clo. NR3—5E 13
Lit. John Rd. NR4—5C 18
Lit. London St. NR2—6E 13
Lit. Melton La. NR4—3A 16
Lit. Melton Rd. NR9—2G 21
Livingstone St. NR2—5A 12
Lloyd Rd. NR1—5H 13
Lloyd Rd. NR8—1C 2
Loanin, The. NR1—3F 19
Lobster La. NR2—6D 12
Locksley Rd. NR4—6C 18
Loddon Rd. NR14—4H 19
Lodge Breck. NR8—3G 3
Lodge La. NR6—4A 6
Lodge Pl. NR7—6C 14
Lodore Av. NR6—4E 5
Loke, The. NR4—6G 17
Loke, The. NR5—2A 10
(Costessey)
Loke, The. NR5—5G 11
(Earlham Rise)
Lollards Rd. NR1—6G 13
London St. NR2—6E 13
Lone Barn Rd. NR7—2H 13
Longbow Clo. NR4—5C 18
Longdell Hills. NR5—2A 10
Long Dri. NR8—1D 2
Longe Rd. NR6—4B 6
Longfields Rd. NR7—4E 15
Long John Hill. NR1—4F 19
Long La. NR2—3B 22
Long La. NR9 & NR5—4F 9
Longmead. NR1—4E 19
Long Row. NR3—3D 12
Longview. NR9—2G 21
Longwater La. NR8 & NR5—1H 9
Lorraine Gdns. NR3—1E 13
Losinga Cres. NR3—1B 12
Lothian St. NR2—6C 12
Louis Clo. NR6—4H 5

Lound Rd. NR4—1H 17
Lovelace Rd. NR4—2G 17
Lovett Clo. NR6—4B 6
Lwr. Clarence Rd. NR1—1G 19
Lower Clo. NR1—6F 13
Lwr. Goat La. NR2—4B 22
Lowes Yd. NR3—2C 22
Low Rd. NR8 & NR6—3G 3
Low Rd. NR13—3G 15
Lowry Cole Rd. NR6—5B 6
Lowther Rd. NR4—5B 18
Lox Wood. NR6—3C 4
Lubbock Clo. NR2—1H 17
Lucerne Clo. NR6—6B 6
Luke Clo. NR5—3B 10
Lusher Rise. NR6—4F 11
Lusher's Loke. NR7—6B 6
Lushington Clo. NR5—4D 10
Lyhart Rd. NR4—5B 18
Lynch Grn. NR9—3G 21
Lyngate Clo. NR9—4E 21
Lytton Rd. NR2—2D 2

Mack's La. NR8—3D 2
Magdalen Clo. NR3—4E 13
Magdalen Rd. NR3—4E 13
Magdalen St. NR3—4E 13
Magnay Rd. NR8—3A 4
Magpie Rd. NR3—4D 12
Maida Vale. NR2—1B 18
Maid Marian Rd. NR4—5C 18
Maidstone Rd. NR1—6E 13
Malbrook Rd. NR5—6D 10
Mallory Rd. NR6—4H 5
Malthouse Rd. NR2—1D 18
Malthouse Rd. NR9—3F 21
Malvern Rd. NR1—6G 13
Malzy Ct. NR3—1B 22
Manby Rd. NR3—3A 14
Manchester Pl. NR2—1C 18
Mancroft Wlk. NR2—5C 12
Mandells Ct. NR3—3C 22
Mansel Dri. NR6—1E 13
Mansfield La. NR1—4E 19
Mantle Clo. NR7—6F 7
Maple Dri. NR2—5H 11
Maple Rd. NR8—1B 2
Margaret Clo. NR6—5B 4
Margaret Cres. NR7—5D 14
Margaret Paston Av. NR3
—3B 12
Margaret Rd. NR5—2D 10
Margetson Av. NR7—5A 14
Mariners La. NR1—2E 19
Marion Rd. NR1—6G 13
Marion Roberts Ct. NR9—4F 21
Marionville Rd. NR3—1E 13
Marjorie Hinde Ct. NR2—5A 23
Market Av. NR1—1E 19
Market La. NR9—1E 21
Markham Tower. NR3—2A 12
Marlborough Ho. NR1—8A 23
Marlborough Rd. NR3—4E 13
Marlingford Rd. NR9—3A 8
Marlingford Way. NR9—2B 8
Marlow Clo. NR1—1E 13
Marl Pit La. NR5—4E 11
Marriot Clo. NR2—5C 12
Marryat Rd. NR7—3A 14
Marshall Clo. NR5—4D 10
Marshall Clo. NR10—5C 20
Marshall Rd. NR3—1B 12
Marston La. NR4—6H 17
Martin Clo. NR7—6D 6
Martineau La. NR1—4F 19
Mary Chapman Ct. NR3—3B 22
Mason Rd. NR6—1C 12
Massingham Rd. NR3—3E 13
Matlock Rd. NR1—1H 19
Maud St. NR2—6B 12
Mayes Clo. NR5—4D 10
Mayfield Av. NR6—6F 5
Mayton Av. NR12—1C 20

Meadowbrook Clo. NR1—3F 19
Meadow Clo. NR5—2C 10
Meadow Clo. NR6—5E 5
Meadow Clo. NR9—4F 21
Meadow Clo. NR14—4H 19
Meadow Gdns. NR6—1F 13
Meadow La. NR7—6D 14
Meadow Rise Av. NR2—2A 18
Meadow Rise Clo. NR2—2A 18
Meadow Rise Rd. NR2—2A 18
Meadow Rd. NR5—2C 10
Meadow Way. NR6—5D 4
Melrose Rd. NR4—3A 18
Melton Ct. NR9—3F 21
Melton Rd. NR9—3F 21
Mendham Clo. NR1—4E 19
Meredith Rd. NR6—4C 4
Merlin Av. NR7—6E 7
Merlin M. NR7—6E 7
Merrow Gdns. NR4—6H 17
Merton Rd. NR2—5A 12
Meteor Clo. NR6—3H 5
Mews, The. NR2—2C 18
Middle Rd. NR13—3G 15
Middleton Clo. NR3—1C 12
Middleton Cres. NR5—2B 10
Middleton's Ct. NR6—6C 4
Middleton's La. NR6—6C 4
Midland St. NR2—5C 12
Mile Cross La. NR6—6F 5
Mile Cross Rd. NR3 & NR2
—3B 12
Mile End Rd. NR4—3A 18
Milestone Clo. NR5—2B 10
Milford Rd. NR2—1B 18
Mill Clo. NR1—3E 19
Mill Clo. NR9—4F 21
Millcroft. NR3—2E 13
Mill Croft Clo. NR5—3A 10
Miller's Breck. NR8—1D 2
Millers La. NR3—3D 12
Mill Hill Rd. NR2—1B 18
Mill La. NR3—4E 13
Mill Rd. NR9—4F 21
(Hethersett)
Mill Rd. NR9—5A 8
(Marlingford)
Mill Rd. NR12—1B 20
Mills Clo. NR8—1C 2
Milton Clo. NR1—3E 19
Milverton Rd. NR1—3F 19
Mitchell Ct. NR5—4B 10
Mitre Ct. NR3—1A 12
Monastery, The. NR3—6E 13
Mons Av. NR1—4G 13
Montcalm Rd. NR1—6H 13
Montgomery Clo. NR5—5B 10
Moore Av. NR6—5B 6
Moorland Clo. NR7—2G 13
Morello Clo. NR1—1G 17
Morgan Way. NR5—4B 10
Morley St. NR3—4F 13
Mornington Rd. NR2—2A 18
Morris Clo. NR5—4C 10
Morse Av. NR1—5A 14
Morse Rd. NR1—5A 14
Mossfield Clo. NR1—4H 13
Mottram Clo. NR5—6F 11
Motum Rd. NR5—5E 11
Mounteney Clo. NR6—6B 6
Mountergate. NR1—1F 19
Mountfield Av. NR6—6D 4
Mt. Pleasant. NR2—2B 18
Mousehold Av. NR3—4F 13
Mousehold Ho. NR1—6H 13
Mousehold La. NR7—2G 13
Mousehold St. NR3—4F 13
Mulberry Clo. NR2—3A 22
Munnings Rd. NR7—3B 14
Muriel Kenny Ct. NR9—4F 21
Muriel Rd. NR2—2A 18
Music Ho. La. NR1—1F 19
Musley Ct. NR2—3B 18
Muspole St. NR3—5D 12

Myrtle Av. NR8—1B 10
Myrtle Rd. NR9—3F 21

Nanthorpe Clo. NR1—5E 19
Napier Pl. NR2—5C 12
Nasmith Rd. NR4—4G 17
Naylor Rd. NR3—3H 11
Nelson St. NR2—5B 12
Netherwood Grn. NR1—4F 19
Neville Clo. NR7—1F 13
Neville Rd. NR7—1F 13
Neville St. NR2—1C 18
Newbegin Clo. NR1—5A 14
Newbegin Rd. NR1—5H 13
Newfound Dri. NR4—5E 17
Newmarket Rd. NR4 & NR2
—6D 16
Newmarket St. NR2—2C 18
New Mills Yd. NR3—5D 12
New Rd. NR9—6F 9
(Bawburgh)
New Rd. NR9—4E 21
(Hethersett)
Newton Clo. NR4—5C 18
Newton Clo. NR14—4H 19
Neylond Cres. NR6—4C 4
Nightingale Cotts. NR1—3F 19
Nightingale Dri. NR8—1B 2
Nightingale La. NR3—4E 13
Nile St. NR2—5B 12
Ninhams Ct. NR2—5A 23
Ninham St. NR1—4E 19
Noble Clo. NR7—3B 14
Noot All. NR5—5D 10
Norfolk St. NR2—1C 18
Norgate Rd. NR4—3G 17
Norgate Way. NR8—2E 3
Normandie Tower. NR1—7E 23
Norman Dri. NR6—3A 6
Norman Rd. NR3—3H 11
Normans Bldgs. NR1—1E 19
Norris Ct. NR3—3C 22
Northcote Rd. NR3—3E 13
Northfields. NR4—2G 17
N. Gage Clo. NR7—6E 7
Northgate. NR6—5D 4
N. Park Av. NR3—3G 17
Northumberland St. NR2—5B 12
Northview Rd. NR5—3E 11
N. Walsham Rd. NR6 & NR12
—6B 6
Norton Dri. NR4—5A 18
Norvic Dri. NR4—4G 17
Norwich Rd. NR5—2D 10
Norwich Rd. NR9 & NR4
—6E 21 & 6A 16
Norwich Rd. NR10—1F 5
Norwich Rd. NR13—1H 15
Notkyin St. NR5—4C 10
Notridge Rd. NR5—5C 10
Nursery Clo. NR6—5C 4
Nursery La. NR8—6F 3
Nutfield Clo. NR4—5G 17

Oak Av. NR7—4D 14
Oak Clo. NR5—2B 10
Oakfields Clo. NR4—6G 17
Oakfields Rd. NR4—6F 17
Oaklands Dri. NR4—5E 17
Oak La. NR3 & NR6—1D 12
Oak Lodge. NR7—6A 14
Oak St. NR3—5D 12
Oaktree Dri. NR7—2H 13
Octagon Clo. NR3—5E 13
*Old Bank of England Ct. NR3
—4C 22*
Old Barge Yd. NR1—1F 19
Old Farm La. NR3—3B 12
Old Gro. Ct. NR3—2D 12
Old Lakenham Hall Dri. NR1
—5E 19
Old Meeting Ho. All. NR3—2C 22

Old Pal. Rd. NR2—5B 12
Old Post Office Ct. NR2—4C 22
Old Post Office Yd. NR2—6E 13
Old Rectory Clo. NR7—6C 14
Olive Clo. NR5—3E 11
Olive Rd. NR5—2D 10
One Post All. NR2—6B 23
Onley St. NR2—2B 18
Opie St. NR2—6E 13
Orchard Bank. NR8—2F 3
Orchard Clo. NR7—4A 14
Orchard Rd. NR10—4C 20
Orchard St. NR2—5C 12
Orchard Way. NR9—3G 21
Orford Hill. NR1—5C 23
Orford Pl. NR2—5C 23
Orford St. NR1—5C 23
Orwell Rd. NR2—3C 18
Osbert Clo. NR1—5E 19
Osborne Rd. NR4—4G 17
Oulton Rd. NR6—5G 5
Oval Av. NR5—3E 11
Oval Rd. NR5—3E 11
Overbury Rd. NR6—6E 5
Overstone Ct. NR6—5B 6
Oxford St. NR2—1C 18
Oxnead Rd. NR3—2B 12

Paddocks, The. NR6—3B 6
Paddock St. NR2—4C 12
Page Rd. NR3—3H 11
Paine Rd. NR7—4B 14
Palace St. NR3—6E 13
Palgrave Clo. NR8—1B 2
Palmer Clo. NR3—2C 12
Palmer Rd. NR3—2C 12
Paradise Pl. NR1—1E 19
Paragon Pl. NR2—6C 12
Parana Rd. NR7—5E 7
Parana Ct. NR7—5E 7
Parana Rd. NR7—5E 7
Park Clo. NR6—5A 6
Park Clo. NR9—4G 21
Park Dri. NR9—4F 21
Parker Rd. NR2—1B 18
Parkers Clo. NR9—2C 8
Parkland Cres. NR6—1F 13
Parkland Rd. NR6—1F 13
Parklands. NR8—6D 2
Park La. NR2—6B 12
Park Rd. NR3—3A 12
Park Rd. NR10—6B 20
Parkside Dri. NR6—5A 6
Park Way. NR6—5C 4
Parmenter Rd. NR4—3H 17
Parsonage Sq. NR2—4C 22
Parsons Mead. NR4—5H 17
Partridge Way. NR6—6H 5
Patricia Rd. NR1—3D 18
Patteson Rd. NR3—4D 12
Peacock St. NR3—5E 13
Pearcefield. NR3—2E 13
Peckover Rd. NR4—4G 17
Peel M. NR2—3A 22
Pelham Rd. NR3—3D 12
Pembrey Clo. NR3—1D 12
Pembroke Rd. NR2—1B 18
Penn Clo. NR8—2D 2
Penn Gro. NR3—3C 12
Penn Rd. NR8—2D 2
Pennyroyal. NR6—5H 5
Penryn Clo. NR4—5H 17
Penshurst M. NR4—5H 17
Percival Clo. NR4—2G 17
Peregrine Clo. NR7—6E 7
Peregrine M. NR7—6E 7
Peregrine Rd. NR7—6E 7
Peterkin Rd. NR4—6C 18
Peterson Rd. NR3—2B 12
Pettus Rd. NR4—3G 17
Peverell Rd. NR5—5C 10
Phelps Rd. NR7—5D 14
Philadelphia La. NR3—2D 12

Pigg La. NR3—6E 13
Pilling Pk. Rd. NR1—5H 13
Pilling Rd. NR7—5B 14
Pinder Clo. NR3—3A 12
Pinder Rd. NR3—3A 12
Pine Clo. NR4—3A 18
Pine Rd. NR7—3C 14
Pinewood Clo. NR6—6D 4
Pioneer Rd. NR6—4C 6
Piper Rd. NR7—3C 14
Pippin Grn. NR4—1G 17
Pitchford Rd. NR5—6E 11
Pitt St. NR3—5D 12
Plaford Rd. NR7—2G 13
Plantation Rd. NR6—4C 4
Plantation, The. NR2—2B 18
Plantsman Clo. NR3—3B 18
Players Way. NR6—4A 6
Pleasant Clo. NR6—5B 4
Plumstead Rd. NR1—5H 13
Plumstead Rd. NR13—2F 15
Plumstead Rd. E. NR7—4B 14
Pockthorpe Ga. NR3—5G 13
Pond Clo. NR9—5F 21
Pond La. NR8—2F 3
Poplar Av. NR4—5G 17
Poplar Clo. NR5—2A 10
Porson Rd. NR7—3A 14
Portersfield Rd. NR2—1B 18
Porter's Loke. NR7—1G 13
Portland St. NR2—1B 18
Portway Pl. NR2—5B 12
Portway Sq. NR2—5C 12
Post Mill Clo. NR7—1F 13
Post Office Rd. NR12—1C 20
Pottergate. NR2—6D 12
Pound La. NR7—3E 15
Press La. NR3—3C 12
Primrose Cres. NR7—6E 15
Primrose Pl. NR2—2B 18
Primrose Rd. NR1—6G 13
Primula Dri. NR4—1G 17
Prince Andrew's Clo. NR6—5F 5
Prince Andrew's Rd. NR6—5F 5
Prince of Wales Rd. NR1—6E 13
Princes St. NR3—6E 13
Prior Rd. NR7—3E 15
Priory Rd. NR9—4G 21
Priscilla Clo. NR5—6F 11
Proctor Rd. NR6—4B 6
Providence Pl. NR1—6G 13
Pudding La. NR2—5B 23
Purland Rd. NR7—2B 14
Puritngay Clo. NR4—5A 18
Pye's Yd. NR3—5E 13
Pyrford Dri. NR4—5H 17

Quaker La. NR10—1A 6
Quakers La. NR3—1B 22
Quay Side. NR3—5E 13
Quebec Rd. NR1—6G 13
Queens Clo. NR4—3A 18
Queen's Rd. NR1—2D 18
Queen's Rd. NR9—3G 21
Queen St. NR3—6E 13

Rachel Clo. NR5—1E 17
Rackham Rd. NR3—2D 12
Raglan St. NR2—6C 12
Railway Cotts. NR1—2G 19
Rampant Horse St. NR2—1D 18
Ramsey Clo. NR4—3G 17
Randle Grn. NR5—4E 11
Randolf Rd. NR1—4E 19
Rangoon Clo. NR7—5E 7
Ranson Rd. NR1—1H 19
Ranworth Rd. NR5—5F 11
Raven Yd. NR1—5D 23
Rawley Rd. NR5—4C 10
Raymond Clo. NR6—3C 4
Raymond Rd. NR6—4D 4
Raynham St. NR2—4C 12

Rayns Clo. NR6—5B 6
Recorder Rd. NR1—6F 13
Recreation Ground Rd. NR7
—6C 6
Recreation Rd. NR2—1A 18
Recreation Rd. NR9—4F 21
Rectory Ct. NR3—2D 12
Red Bri. La. NR5—2E 11
Red Cottage Clo. NR3—2A 12
Redfern Clo. NR7—3C 14
Redfern Rd. NR7—3B 14
Red Lion St. NR1—1E 19
Redmere Clo. NR12—1C 20
Redwell St. NR2—6E 13
Reepham Rd. NR8 & NR6—1H 3
Regina Rd. NR1—2D 18
Reydon Clo. NR5—5C 10
Rice Clo. NR7—2A 14
Richardson Cres. NR9—3F 21
Richenda Clo. NR5—1E 17
Richmond Rd. NR5—3A 10
Rider Haggard Rd. NR7—3A 14
Ridgeway, The. NR1—4A 14
Ridings, The. NR4—6F 17
Riley Clo. NR7—3B 14
Rimington Rd. NR7—6C 6
Ringland La. NR8—4A 2
Ringland Rd. NR8—1A 2
Ringland Rd. NR9—1A 8
Ring Rd. NR7—5C 14
Ripley Clo. NR2—1H 17
Riseway Clo. NR1—4H 13
River La. NR3—5F 13
Riverside. NR1—1F 19
Riverside Clo. NR6—2F 11
Riverside Rd. NR1—6F 13
Robberds Way. NR5—4A 10
Robert Gybson Way. NR2—6D 12
Robin Hood Rd. NR4—5C 18
Robson Rd. NR5—6D 10
Rocelin Clo. NR3—1E 13
Rockingham Rd. NR5—6E 11
Rockland Dri. NR7—6A 14
Roedich Dri. NR8—1C 2
Rogers Clo. NR5—5D 10
Rolleston Clo. NR5—5D 10
Romany Rd. NR3—3F 13
Ropemakers Row. NR3—3C 12
Rosa Clo. NR10—6D 20
Rosary Rd. NR1—6G 13
Roseacre Clo. NR7—2A 14
Rose Av. NR1—1E 19
Rosebay Clo. NR6—5H 5
Rosebery Rd. NR3—3D 12
Rosedale Cres. NR1—6G 13
Rose La. NR1—1E 19
Rosemary La. NR3—5D 12
Rosemary Rd. NR7—6D 6
Rosetta Rd. NR10—5D 20
Rose Valley. NR2—1B 18
Roseville Rd. NR1—1H 19
Rosslare. NR2—2E 13
Rossons Rd. NR8—1C 2
Rostwold Way. NR3—2D 12
Rotary Ct. NR6—2G 11
Rouen Rd. NR1—1E 19
Roundtree Clo. NR7—2H 13
Roundtree Way. NR7—2H 13
Roundwell Rd. NR5—3H 9
Rowington Rd. NR1—2D 18
Rowland Ct. NR1—2E 19
Roxley Clo. NR7—6D 14
Royal Arc. NR2—5C 23
Royal Oak Ct. NR1—6D 23
Rugge Dri. NR4—4G 17
Runcton Clo. NR5—5D 10
Rupert St. NR2—2C 18
(in two parts)
Rushmore Clo. NR7—5C 6
Rushmore Rd. NR7—5C 6
Ruskin Rd. NR4—2G 17
Ruskin Rd. NR5—3D 10
Russell Av. NR7—1H 13

Russell Av. NR10—5C 20
Russell St. NR2—5C 12
Russell Ter. NR14—4H 19
Russett Gro. NR4—1G 17
Rutland St. NR2—2C 18
Rydal Clo. NR5—6E 11
Rye Av. NR3—1B 12
Rye Clo. NR3—2B 12
Ryrie Ct. NR4—4H 17

Sadler Rd. NR6—3D 4
Saffron Sq. NR3—1C 12
St Alban's Rd. NR1—3D 18
St Andrew's Av. NR7—6E 15
St Andrew's Clo. NR7—6E 15
St Andrew's Dri. NR4—6G 17
St Andrew's Hill. NR2—6E 13
St Andrew's Plain. NR3—3C 22
St Andrew's Rd. NR6—4B 4
St Andrew's St. NR2—6E 13
St Ann La. NR1—1F 19
St Augustine's St. NR3—4D 12
St Bartholomew's Clo. NR2
—4B 12
St Benedict's St. NR2—6D 12
St Catherine's Clo. NR1—2E 19
St Catherine's Plain. NR1—8D 23
St Catherine's Rd. NR7—4D 14
St Clement's All. NR3—2C 22
St Clement's Hill. NR3—2E 13
St Crispin's Rd. NR3—5D 12
St David's Rd. NR9—5F 21
St Edmund's Clo. NR6—3G 11
St Edmund's Clo. NR8—5F 3
St Edmund's Rise. NR8—2C 2
St Edmund's Rd. NR8—1C 2
St Faith's La. NR1—6E 13
St Faith's Rd. NR6 & NR10
—6H 5
St George's All. NR3—2B 22
St George's St. NR3—5D 12
St Giles Ter. NR2—4A 22
St Giles St. NR2—6D 12
St Gregory's All. NR2—4B 22
St Helen's Sq. NR1—5F 13
St James Clo. NR3—5D 12
St John Maddermarket. NR2
—6D 12
St John's All. NR2—4B 22
St John's Clo. NR1—4E 19
St John's Clo. NR9—5F 21
St Julian's All. NR1—1E 19
St Lawrence Clo. NR2—4A 22
St Lawrence Dri. NR4—5E 17
St Lawrence La. NR2—6D 12
*St Lawrence Lit. Steps. NR2
—3A 22*
St Leonard's Rd. NR1—6G 13
St Margaret's All. NR2—3A 22
St Margaret's St. NR2—6D 12
St Martin-at-Palace Plain. NR3
—5E 13
*St Martin's at Oak Wall La. NR3
—1A 22*
St Martin's Clo. NR3—4D 12
St Martin's La. NR3—5D 12
St Martin's Rd. NR3—4D 12
St Mary's All. NR3—2B 22
St Mary's Plain. NR3—5D 12
St Mary's Rd. NR3—4D 12
St Matthew's Rd. NR1—6F 13
*St Maichael at Pleas Ct. NR3
—3D 22*
St Mildred's Rd. NR5—6D 10
St Miles All. NR3—2B 22
St Olave's Rd. NR3—4E 13
St Paul's Clo. NR6—5E 5
St Paul's Opening. NR3—5E 13
St Paul's Sq. NR3—1D 22
St Peter's Clo. NR4—6F 17
St Peter's St. NR2—1D 18
St Peter's Way. NR10—5C 20
St Philip's Clo. NR2—6B 12

St Philip's Rd. NR2—6B 12
St Saviour's All. NR3—1C 22
St Saviour's La. NR3—5E 13
St Simon Ct. NR3—3D 22
St Stephen's Rd. NR1—2D 18
St Stephen's Sq. NR1—2D 18
St Stephen's St. NR1—1D 18
St Swithin's All. NR2—3A 22
St Swithin's Rd. NR2—6D 12
St Thomas Rd. NR2—6A 12
St Vedast St. NR1—6F 13
St Walstan's Clo. NR5—3H 9
St Walstan's Clo. NR8—2D 2
St Walstan's Rd. NR8—1D 2
St William's Way. NR7—5B 14
Sale Rd. NR7—2B 14
Salhouse Rd. NR7 & NR13 —2A 14
Salisbury Rd. NR1—1H 19
Salter Av. NR4—1G 17
Samson Rd. NR6—6D 4
Samuel Rd. NR1—4H 13
Sandholme Clo. NR1—4H 13
Sandringham Ct. NR2—8A 23
Sandringham Rd. NR2—6B 12
Sandy La. NR1—6E 19
Sandy La. NR4—5D 18
Sandy La. NR8—1C 2
Saracen Rd. NR6—4D 4
Saunders Ct. NR1—6G 13
Savery Clo. NR5—6D 10
Sawyers Clo. NR5—3A 10
Sayers St. NR2—5C 12
Scarlet Rd. NR4—5D 18
Scarnell Rd. NR5—6F 11
Sceptre Clo. NR6—1A 12
School Av. NR7—6D 14
School La. NR2—4C 22
School La. NR7—6B 6
(Sprowston)
School La. NR7—6B 14
(Thorpe St Andrew)
School Rd. NR8—1F 3
School Rd. NR12—1C 20
School Ter. NR14—4H 19
Scotch Hill Rd. NR8—1C 2
Seaman Tower. NR3—2A 12
Sego Vale. NR8—2E 3
Seton Rd. NR8—1E 3
Sewell Rd. NR3—2E 13
Shakespeare Way. NR8—2D 2
Sheep Meadow Clo. NR5—3A 10
Shelley Dri. NR8—2D 2
Shepherd Clo. NR5—1F 17
Sherbourne Pl. NR1—1F 19
Sheridan Clo. NR8—2F 3
Sherwell Rd. NR6—4C 4
Sherwood Rd. NR4—5C 18
Shipfield. NR3—1F 13
Shipstone Rd. NR3—4E 13
Shirley Clo. NR12—1C 20
Shooters Clo. NR8—1D 2
Shop La. NR9—3H 21
Shorncliffe Av. NR3—3B 12
Shorncliffe Clo. NR3—3C 12
Sidney Rd. NR8—6F 3
Sienna M. NR1—5H 13
Sigismund Rd. NR1—3D 18
Silver Rd. NR3—3F 13
Silver St. NR3—4E 13
Skelton Rd. NR7—4A 14
Skoner Rd. NR8—1E 3
Skye Clo. NR5—4C 10
Sleaford Grn. NR3—2C 12
Smeat St. NR5—5D 10
Smee Rd. NR13—4H 15
Smithdale Rd. NR5—3D 10
Smithfield Rd. NR1—3F 19
Softley Dri. NR4—4E 17
Soleme Rd. NR3—3B 12
Somerleyton Gdns. NR2—1C 18
Somerleyton St. NR2—1C 18
Somerset Way. NR8—1B 2
Sorrel Ho. NR5—4C 10

South Av. NR7—6C 14
South Croft. NR9—4F 21
Southerton Rd. NR4—3H 17
Southerwood. NR6—5H 5
S. Gage Clo. NR7—6F 7
Southgate La. NR1—2F 19
S. Hill Clo. NR7—4D 14
S. Hill Rd. NR7—3D 14
S. Park Av. NR3—4G 17
South Wlk. NR13—2F 15
Southwell Rd. NR1—2D 18
Sovereign Way. NR3—5E 13
Sparhawk Av. NR7—6E 7
Sparhawk Clo. NR7—6E 7
Spar Rd. NR6—5G 5
Speke St. NR2—5A 12
Spelman Rd. NR2—2A 18
Spencer Rd. NR3—4E 13
Spencer Rd. NR6—5G 5
Spindle Rd. NR6—6H 5
Spinney Clo. NR7—4D 14
Spinney Rd. NR7—4C 14
Spital Fields. NR1—5G 13
Spitfire Rd. NR6—4G 5
Spixworth Rd. NR6—6A 6
Spixworth Rd. NR10—1A 20
Springbank. NR1—4E 19
(in two parts)
Springfield Rd. NR7—2B 14
Springfield Rd. NR8—1C 2
Sprowston Rd. NR3—3E 13
Spynke Rd. NR3—1B 12
Stacy Rd. NR3—4E 13
Stafford Av. NR5—3B 10
Stafford St. NR2—6B 12
Stamp Office Yd. NR2—3C 22
Stanley Av. NR7—6A 14
Stanmore Clo. NR7—6C 14
Stanmore Rd. NR7—6C 14
Stannard Rd. NR4—1H 17
Stanninghall Rd. NR12—1D 20
Starling Rd. NR3—4D 12
Statham Clo. NR4—4B 18
Station Rd. NR8—3F 3
Steepgreen Clo. NR1—4A 14
Stepping La. NR1—1E 19
Steps, The. NR2—6B 12
Stevenson Rd. NR5—5D 10
Steward St. NR3—4E 13
Stillington Clo. NR7—1H 13
Stocks Hill. NR9—6F 9
Stoke Rd. NR1—5F 19
Stone Breck. NR5—2A 10
Stonehouse Rd. NR7—6D 6
Stone Rd. NR3—3C 12
Stones Bldgs. NR3—3E 13
Stracey Rd. NR1—1G 19
Strangers Ct. NR2—6D 12
Stratford Clo. NR1—4F 19
Stratford Cres. NR5—4E 17
Stratford Dri. NR1—4F 19
Street, The. NR1 & NR14—4H 19
Street, The. NR8—5F 3
(Costessey)
Street, The. NR8—2B 2
(Taverham)
Stuart Clo. NR9—3G 21
Stuart Ct. NR1—4E 22
Stuart Gdns. NR1—4E 22
Stuart Rd. NR1—2F 19
Stylman Rd. NR5—5C 10
Suckling Av. NR3—1B 12
Suckling La. NR9—6H 21
Suffield Clo. NR4—6F 17
Suffield Rd. NR3—2D 12
Suffolk Sq. NR2—1C 18
Sumpter Rd. NR4—3G 17
Suncroft. NR1—4F 19
Sun La. NR3—4E 13
Sunningdale. NR4—4A 18
Sunny Clo. NR5—3D 10
Sunny Gro. NR5—3D 10
Sunny Hill. NR1—4F 19
Supple Rd. NR1—5A 14

Surrey Clo. NR7—5E 7
Surrey Gro. NR1—1E 19
Surrey St. NR1—1E 19
Sursham Av. NR6—6B 6
Sussex St. NR3—5D 12
Sutherland Av. NR6—6E 5
Swafield St. NR5—5B 10
Swan La. NR2—4C 22
Swansea Rd. NR2—1B 18
Sweet Briar Industrial Est. NR3 —3H 11
Sweetbriar La. NR6—3D 6
Sweet Briar Rd. NR6—4H 11
Swinbourne Clo. NR6—1E 13
Sycamore Cres. NR2—5H 11
Sydney Rd. NR10—5C 20
Sywell Clo. NR6—4B 6

Talbot Sq. NR3—5D 12
Taleworth Clo. NR5—5C 10
Tanager Clo. NR3—1D 12
Tanners Ct. NR3—4C 12
Tansy Clo. NR6—6H 5
Taverham Chase. NR8—2D 2
Taverham La. NR8—2B 2
Taverham Rd. NR8—2C 2
Taverners Sq. NR3—1E 22
Taylor Rd. NR5—6E 11
Taylor's La. NR6—4H 5
(in two parts)
Telegraph La. E. NR1—6H 13
Telegraph La. W. NR1—6G 13
Templemere. NR3—2G 13
Temple Rd. NR3—3E 13
Ten Bell Ct. NR2—6C 12
Ten Bell La. NR2—6D 12
Terence Av. NR7—6C 6
Terrace, The. NR1—6G 13
Terrace Wlk. NR1—8D 23
Theatre St. NR2—1D 18
Theobald Rd. NR1—6D 18
Thomas Tawell Ho. NR3—4E 13
Thomas Vere Rd. NR7—5D 14
Thompson Rd. NR7—4D 14
Thompsons Yd. NR3—5E 13
Thor Clo. NR7—5C 14
Thor Loke. NR7—5C 14
Thornham Clo. NR7—2H 13
Thornham Dri. NR7—2H 13
Thornham Rd. NR7—2H 13
Thorn La. NR1—1E 19
Thoroughfare Yd. NR3—2C 22
Thorpe Av. NR7—4C 14
Thorpe Rd. NR7—5D 14
Thorpe Heights. NR1—6G 13
Thorpe M. NR7—6D 14
Thorpe Rd. NR1—1G 19
Thor Rd. NR7—5C 14
Three Corner Dri. NR6—4B 6
Three King La. NR2—6D 12
Three Mile La. NR5—3B 10
Three Towers Ct. NR3—2A 12
Thunder La. NR7—4C 14
Thurling Plain. NR7—3C 14
Thurston Clo. NR4—8A 10
Tiercel Av. NR7—6E 7
Tillett Ct. NR3—2E 13
Tillett Rd. NR3—2E 13
Tillett Rd. E. NR3—2E 13
Tills Clo. NR6—6B 6
Tills Rd. NR6—5C 6
Timberhill. NR1—1E 19
Timothy Clo. NR1—4H 13
Toftes Pl. NR5—4D 10
Tollhouse Rd. NR5—5G 11
Tolwin Wlk. NR3—3F 13
Tombland. NR3—6E 13
Tombland All. NR3—3D 22
Tottington Clo. NR5—4B 10
Tower Clo. NR8—6C 2
Tower Hill. NR7—6B 14
Tower Hill. NR8—6C 2

Towers, The. NR1—8F 23
Town Clo. Rd. NR2—3C 18
Town Ho. Rd. NR8—6E 3
Townsend Rd. NR4—5C 18
Tracey Rd. NR7—3C 14
Trafalgar St. NR1—2E 19
Trafford Rd. NR1—3D 18
Traverse St. NR3—3D 12
Tremaine Clo. NR6—3F 11
Trendall Rd. NR7—6F 7
Trident Rd. NR1—5G 13
Trilithorn Clo. NR6—2F 11
Trinity St. NR2—1C 18
Trix Rd. NR2—2C 18
Trory St. NR2—1C 18
Truman Clo. NR5—1E 17
Tuckswood Centre. NR4—5C 18
Tuckswood La. NR4—4C 18
Tudor Ct. NR1—2E 19
Tunstall Clo. NR5—5C 10
Turner Rd. NR2—5A 12
Turners Sq. NR1—5D 23
Tusser Rd. NR8—2E 3
Tusting Clo. NR7—6B 6

Union St. NR2—2C 18
Unthank Rd. NR2—2B 18
Unthank Rd. NR4—4G 17
Uplands Ct. NR4—3A 18
Up. Breckland Rd. NR5—3B 10
Upper Clo. NR1—6E 13
Up. Goat La. NR2—6D 12
Up. Green La. NR3—5E 13
Up. King St. NR3—6E 13
Up. St Giles St. NR2—6C 12
Up. Stafford Av. NR5—3B 10
Upton Clo. NR4—4A 18
Upton Rd. NR4—3A 18

Vale Grn. NR3—3A 12
Valentine St. NR2—6C 12
Valley Dri., The. NR1—4H 13
Valley Rd. NR5—3E 11
Valley Side Rd. NR1—4A 14
Valley View Cres. NR5—2C 10
Valpy Av. NR3—3A 12
Vancouver Rd. NR4—4A 14
Varvel Av. NR7—6E 7
Varvel Clo. NR7—1A 14
Vauxhall St. NR2—1C 18
Vawdrey Rd. NR8—1F 3
Venables Clo. NR1—5H 13
Vera Rd. NR6—6F 5
Vicarage Clo. NR8—5F 3
Vicarage Ct. NR7—1G 13
Vicarage Rd. NR3—3C 12
Victoria Clo. NR2—2C 2
Victoria Rd. NR8—2C 2
Victoria St. NR1—2D 18
Vincent Rd. NR1—5G 13
Violet Rd. NR3—3F 13
Virginia Clo. NR7—6E 7
Vulcan Rd. INdustrial Est. NR6 —5G 5
Vulcan Rd. N. NR6—5G 5
Vulcan Rd. S. NR6—6G 5

Waddington Ct. NR2—5B 12
Waddington St. NR2—5B 12
Wades Yd. NR3—4D 22
Waggon & Horses La. NR3 —6E 13
Wakefield Rd. NR5—6E 11
Wakehurst Clo. NR4—5H 17
Walcot Clo. NR5—5D 10
Waldeck Rd. NR4—3A 18
Weldegrave. NR5—4C 10
Waldemar Av. NR6—5F 5
Waldemar Pk. NR6—5F 5
Wall Rd. NR3—2E 13
Walnuts, The. NR4—4B 18

Walpole Gdns. NR2—5A 23
Walpole St. NR2—1C 18
Walters Rd. NR8—2D 2
Walton Rd. NR1—3E 19
Ward La. NR1—1H 19
Waring Rd. NR5—6D 10
Warnett Rd. NR7—3B 14
Warren Av. NR6—5E 5
Warren Clo. NR6—6A 6
Warren, The. NR6—6A 6
Warwick St. NR2—1B 18
Watering, The. NR3—4C 12
Water La. NR3—6D 12
Water La. NR4—5E 17
Water La. NR7—6B 14
Waterloo Pk. Av. NR3—3C 12
Waterloo Pk. Clo. NR3—3C 12
Weterloo Rd. NR3—4D 12
Waterman Rd. NR2—5H 11
Waterside. NR1—5F 13
Waterworks Rd. NR2—5A 12
Watkin Rd. NR4—6C 18
Watling Rd. NR7—3B 14
Watlings Ct. NR2—4A 22
Watson Gro. NR2—4B 12
Watton Rd. NR9 & NR4—2A 16
Watts Ct. NR2—5A 23
Waverley Rd. NR4—4A 18
Weavers La. NR2—5B 23
Webdell Ct. NR1—5F 19
Webster Clo. NR5—4D 10
Wellesley Av. N. NR1—5H 13
Wellesley Av. S. NR1—6H 13
Wellington La. NR2—6C 12
Wellington Rd. NR2—6B 12
Well Loke. NR3—1B 12
Wells Grn. NR12—1C 20
Welsford Rd. NR4—5B 18
Wendene. NR5—5B 10
Wenman Ct. NR5—4B 10

Wensum Cres. NR6—1F 11
Wensum St. NR3—6E 13
Wensum Valley Clo. NR6—6A 4
Wentworth Grn. NR4—4A 18
Werningham Rd. NR6—4A 6
Wessex St. NR2—1D 18
Westacre Dri. NR6—3A 6
West Clo. NR5—2C 10
West Croft. NR9—4F 21
West End. NR8—5C 2
West End Av. NR8—5C 2
W. End St. NR2—5B 12
Western Av. NR7—6C 14
Westgate. NR6—5D 4
Westgate Clo. NR2—2A 18
Westlegate. NR1—1E 19
Weston Ct. NR6—4B 6
Weston Rd. NR3 & NR6—1C 12
Weston Wood Clo. NR7—6C 14
Weston Wood Rd. NR7—6B 14
West Pde. NR2—6B 12
W. Pottergate. NR2—6C 12
West Rd. NR5—2C 10
Westwick St. NR2—6D 12
Westwood Dri. NR6—4B 4
Westwood Ho. NR2—6A 12
Wheatley Rd. NR2—5H 11
Wheeler Rd. NR3—3A 12
Whiffler Rd. NR3—1A 12
Whitebeam Ct. NR5—5F 11
White Farm La. NR7—6A 14
Whitefriars. NR3—5E 13
White Gates. NR5—3A 10
Whitegates Clo. NR9—4G 21
Whitehall Rd. NR2—1B 18
White Horse La. NR14—6F 19
White Ho. Ct. NR3—1C 12
White Lion St. NR2—1E 19
Whitethorn Clo. NR6—5H 5
White Woman La. NR6—4B 6

Whiting Rd. NR4—5D 18
Whitlingham La. NR7—6D 14
Whitlingham La. NR14—4H 19
Whitwell Rd. NR1—5G 13
Wilberforce Rd. NR5—6D 10
Wilby Rd. NR1—5E 19
Wild Rd. NR3—3D 12
Willhire Way. NR6—4F 5
William Booth St. NR2—1D 18
William Mear Gdns. NR1—6H 13
William Peck Rd. NR10—5B 20
William's Loke. NR7—4B 14
Williamson Clo. NR7—2A 14
Willis St. NR3—5E 13
Willow La. NR2—6D 12
Winchcomb Rd. NR2—5H 11
Windmill Ct. NR3—2G 13
Windmill La. NR8—6G 3
Windmill Rd. NR3—2F 13
Windsor Rd. NR6—4D 4
Wingate Way. NR2—5C 12
Wingfield Rd. NR3—4D 12
Winkles Row. NR1—8F 23
Winsford Way. NR6—3E 11
Winter Rd. NR2—6A 12
Witard Clo. NR7—3B 14
Witard Rd. NR7—3B 14
Woburn St. NR2—1C 18
Wodehouse St. NR3—4E 13
Wolfe Rd. NR1—5H 13
Womersley Clo. NR1—5H 13
Womersley Rd. NR1—5H 13
Woodcock Clo. NR3—1D 12
Woodcock Rd. NR3—1C 12
Woodcroft Clo. NR7—2C 14
Woodforde Rd. NR7—2B 14
Woodham Leas. NR6—4A 6
Wood Hill. NR8—2D 2
Woodhill Rise. NR5—4E 11
Woodland Clo. NR6—4B 4

Woodland Dri. NR6—4A 6
Woodland Dri. NR13—2F 15
Woodland Rd. NR6—4B 4
Woodlands Cres. NR7—3E 15
Woodlands Rd. NR5—2C 10
Woodrow Pl. NR1—6H 13
Woodruff Clo. NR6—5H 5
Woods Clo. NR9—4F 21
Woodside Clo. NR8—1C 2
Woodside Ct. NR1—3F 19
Woodside Rd. NR7—2C 14
Wood St. NR1—2D 18
Woodview Ct. NR5—2C 10
Wood View Rd. NR6—5C 4
Woodview Rd. NR9—2A 8
Woodward Rd. NR3—3B 12
Wordsworth Rd. NR5—6E 11
Wortham Clo. NR5—4C 10
Wrench Rd. NR5—6F 11
Wren Clo. NR4—4G 17
Wrights Ct. NR3—3C 22
Wroxham Rd. NR7, NR13 & NR12
—6D 6
Wycliffe Rd. NR4—2G 17
Wymer St. NR2—6C 12

Yare Valley Dri. NR4—4E 17
Yarmouth Rd. NR7 & NR13
—6A 14
Yaxley Way. NR5—5C 10
Yelverton Clo. NR6—5B 4
Yew Ct. NR7—6F 7
York St. NR2—2B 18
(in two parts)

Zipfel's Ct. NR3—1C 22
Zobel Clo. NR3—2H 11

Printed and bound in Great Britain by Halstan & Co. Ltd., Plantation Road, Amersham, Bucks.